POWER AND
PERSONALITY

HAROLD DWIGHT LASSWELL, Ph.D.
PROFESSOR OF LAW, YALE UNIVERSITY LAW SCHOOL

POWER AND PERSONALITY

THE VIKING PRESS · NEW YORK

VIKING COMPASS EDITION
ISSUED IN 1962 BY THE VIKING PRESS. INC.
625 MADISON AVENUE, NEW YORK, N.Y. 10022
DISTRIBUTED IN CANADA
BY THE MACMILLAN COMPANY OF CANADA LIMITED

SBN 670-00101-5

THIS EDITION PUBLISHED BY ARRANGEMENT
WITH W. W. NORTON & COMPANY, INC.
FIFTH PRINTING NOVEMBER 1969

PRINTED IN THE U.S.A. BY THE MURRAY PRINTING COMPANY

CONTENTS

5

I. INTRODUCTION:
THE MEANING OF POWER

THE MUTUAL impact of power and personality is a topic of enduring human interest. The often bitter fruit of experience is distilled in maxims of folk wisdom, and in rhymes, aphorisms and declarations of poets, philosophers and scholars. As Samuel Butler has it, "Authority intoxicates,"

> The fumes of it invade the brain,
> And make men giddy, proud, and vain. (1) *

Henry Adams' education taught him that "the effect of power and publicity on all men is the aggravation of self, a sort of tumor that ends by killing the victim's sympathies," and "a friend in power is a friend lost." (2) "There is something in politics which degrades," observes a recent writer, echoing an old complaint. "They turn good men into bad men, and bad men into worse." (3)

The institutions of society which are specialized to the shaping and sharing of power are freely stigmatized as evil. In Tom Paine's words, "Government, even in its best estate, is but a necessary evil." (4) There is the memorable distinction made by William Godwin between society and government, society being produced by our "wants" and government by our "wickedness." (5) And Friedrich Engels

* Figures in parentheses refer to Notes in back of book.

7

in his attack upon the state held that the essential fact about the state, as about religion, is the "anxiety of mankind before itself." (6)

To complete the indictment of power and government, we are often told that only the corrupted seek power. An early and unfavorable comparison of the politician to the magician has been repeated across the centuries. Philo Judaeus lived at Alexandria during the first century of our era, and in a treatise on dreams classifies the art of politics along with that of magic. He compares Joseph's coat of many colors to "the much-variegated web of political affairs" where along with "the smallest possible portion of truth" falsehoods of every shade of plausibility are interwoven. He compares politicians and statesmen to augurs, ventriloquists and sorcerers, "men skillful in juggling and in incantations and in tricks of all kinds, from whose treacherous arts it is very difficult to escape." Philo adds that Moses very naturally represented Joseph's coat as stained with blood, since all statecraft is tainted with wars and bloodshed.

Twelve centuries later Moses Maimonides in his *Guide for the Perplexed* cites this passage, and Albertus Magnus adds his commentary. In some men, writes Albert, the intellect is abundant and active and clear. These men are akin to such superior substances as the angels and stars, and therefore Maimonides is correct in calling them sages. But there are others who, according to Albert, confound true wisdom with sophistry and are content with mere probabilities and imaginations and are at home in "rhetorical and civil matters." Maimonides described this class as one in which the imaginative faculty preponderates while the rational faculty is imperfect. "Whence arises the sect of politicians, of legislators, of diviners, of enchanters, of dreamers . . . and of prestidigiteurs who work marvels of strange cunning and occult arts." (7)

But the term power has a semantic coat of many colors, not all of which are symbols of evil portent. Power, it is conceded, can be wielded for worthy purposes by the strong and good. Even those who hold that power is evil do not call all who use it evildoers. On the contrary some of the men of power are among the culture heroes of mankind, the "great men" of history, the "lawgivers," "liberators" and "nation founders"; in a word, the statesmen. In this perspective power, government and personality are favorably judged. (8)

The starting point of our present undertaking is neither the praise nor dispraise of the way power and personality interact upon each other. We begin by observing Caesar; later we may bury him. Our aim is to discover whether the recent expansion of the social, psychological and medical sciences has added to our knowledge of power and the power seeker.

It is true that the inquiry is not an end in itself. We have a sociopolitical objective, the more perfect instrumentation of democratic values. When we arrive at a basic analysis of the interplay of personality and power, a further step is the consideration of how to put what we have learned in the service of human dignity. At that point we pass from the contemplative to the manipulative approach, and undertake to devise ways and means of putting power in the service of a democratic society, a society in which power and respect are shared, and in which other values are made more abundant and accessible to all. Hence we consider the problem of democratic leadership, of the democratic elite. We come to it after we have explored the political type in general and in some of its special manifestations.

The accent is on power and the powerful. But it would be a mistake to imagine that in consequence we are wholly taken up with the few rather than the many. Speaking of power and the powerful is an ellipsis, leaving out what is perhaps the longest arc of the circle constituting a power relation. Power is an interpersonal situation; those who hold power are empowered. They depend upon and continue only so long as there is a continuing stream of empowering responses. Even a casual inspection of human relations will convince any competent observer that power is not a brick that can be lugged from place to place, but a process that vanishes when the supporting responses cease.

CUE GIVE-AND-TAKE

The power relation is give-and-take; or, to give a more dynamic twist to the words, it is giving-and-taking. It is cue-giving and cue-taking in a continuing spiral of interaction. (9)

We shall specialize our meaning in a moment, but it is useful to linger on the empowering-empowered dimension of every interpersonal relation. The flow of activity between two or more interacting persons is guided by the presentation of cues at the focus of attention of the participants. Many situations are so highly specialized that the cue-giving function is concentrated in one person. The conductor is a continuing source of cues at the focus of the orchestra's attention. In the drill group the commanding officer gives the orders. On some jobs the foreman is busy signaling for machinery to be started or stopped, and for other operations to begin or cease.

Although cue-giving is highly concentrated in the conductor, commanding officer or foreman, the function is not wholly monopolized by any one of them. The conductor, for instance, is continuously responsive to what comes to his attention from the orchestra; and neither the drill master nor the foreman is oblivious to the behavior of his men. And the members of the orchestra, the squad or the workteam are attentive to one another, adapting themselves to one another's performance. In many human relationships it is obvious that the giving and receiving of cues is not concentrated in the hands of one participant. In a game of bridge the deal is passed around and in tennis the service alternates; in both games every player is on the alert to every other.

It is possible to "score" various situations according to the characteristic pattern of cue-giving and taking. This can be done by describing the focus of attention of each participant through the entire course of the interaction. We can describe the flow of debate in a legislative body according to the number and length of participations by each member. A more intensive description notes how many members are present or absent during a session, and how many of the members present in the chamber are listening. A yet more intensive procedure would consist of trying to find by careful interviewing which cues were regarded as significant at the time (such as the directions from the party whip or floor leader). (10) A comprehensive account of the situation relates the responses observed to the significant features of the environment to which a responder was exposed, and also to the predispositions with which the responder entered the situation.

The foregoing analysis reminds us, then, that there is a sense in which the conceptions of power (or what is often used synonymously, "leadership") can be applied to every cue-giving and taking relationship. If the circle of cue-taking is not closed, the relationship is broken, and the power relation no longer occurs. (11)

But this analysis is not sufficiently specialized to deal with the phenomena which political science has to consider. Granted that a willful or accidental misreading of the conductor's directions may spoil the performance; granted that an order may be misconstrued or disobeyed on the drill ground; granted that the foreman's signal may be neglected or disregarded. What happens then? The incident may be passed over in silence. Or there may be sharp remonstrance. Perhaps somebody will be cut off the payroll. A fine may be assessed. A soldier may be sent to the guardhouse, subjected to corporal punishment or compulsory labor. In general, we can say that when the pattern of expectations is contradicted in action, deprivations may be imposed. And the deprivations may be included within the original expectation pattern.

THE PATTERN OF EXPECTATION

At this point we narrow our conception of power, using the term to designate relations in which severe deprivations are expected to follow the breach of a pattern of conduct. (12) This eliminates an enormous range of relationships in which a breach is assumed to be of trivial importance.

This mode of conceiving power emphasizes the crucial role of expectation. One conductor may expect to deal strictly with his men, and to impose penalties for minor as well as major deviation from the faithful following of his cues. And an orchestra may expect to deal strictly with conductors if the players are dissatisfied. Indeed, by deliberate non-co-operation or hostile agitation, they may get him fired.

Manifestly, expectations may differ about what constitutes a deprivation, and what is mild or severe. When we are examining not one human association but a whole community, or all the communities of which there is knowledge, we define severity or mildness in the light of the entire panorama of relationships which are taken into account.

When we conceive power in this way, we are close to the traditional understanding of power in the political and legal sciences. (13) Legal and political analyses are made from the perspective of a community within which several forms of human associations are included. And scientific attention is directed toward the institutions that are specialized to threatening or applying the most severe sanctions against aberrant persons.

GOVERNMENT

But it should not be supposed that our conception of power leads only to the county courthouse or state legislature or Capitol Hill, and disregards Wall Street, the National Press Building and the headquarters of the pressure groups organized in the name of business, agriculture, labor, the professions, the veterans, the women or religion. Or even that our narrowed definition necessarily takes us out of the board of directors meeting of corporations, or even out of the industrial plant or local union headquarters. We look for power relations throughout the institutional network of any community; and we are prepared to recognize as power whatever relationships involve the expectation of severe deprivations (as severity is construed by a considerable number of those in the community who are acquainted with such circumstances). The corporation that tries to enforce discipline by shutting down plants or cutting wages or speeding up machines or lengthening hours is imposing a deprivation upon workers, not only from the standpoint of the workers immediately affected, but in the eyes of the employers and other citizens of the community. In the same way a trade union is imposing sanctions when it puts through a plant stoppage or spoils and slows down work or destroys plant property or uses violence against persons who appear ready to take a job. (14)

The conception of power as sanctioned expectation, therefore, often leads us beyond situations conventionally known in a community as "governmental." At the same time, many relationships called governmental may be omitted. But we have the advantage of talking about situations that are functionally, if not conventionally, comparable; and this is essential for scientific purposes. So we hold to the point that government, functionally speaking, comprises the institutions of power; conventionally, government is what is called government in local usage.

Two sets of expectations are found in any given set of circumstances, one pertaining to what people regard as authoritative and the other to what they regard as controlling. A law passed by the Congress and signed by the President in the regular manner is usually expected to be accepted as authoritative by the courts and by private associations and individuals. But this is not true of all statutes. Some of the clauses printed as the code of a given jurisdiction are no longer regarded as authoritative, and any attempt to invoke them would be futile. Thus some statutes are expected to be authoritative and controlling; others are expected to be neither one nor the other. And there are mixed instances in which a rule is plainly admitted to be authoritative but is not expected to be applied in fact (such as certain restrictions on trade practice).

A power situation is defined, then, in terms of expectation. But it is by no means exhausted thereby. For expectations do not occur apart from a more complex perspective. Power holders or those within the domain of power usually entertain goals, plans, justifications and loyalties in addition to simple estimates of what is likely to happen. (And the estimates may be erroneous owing to the influence of bias toward obtaining a desired result.) The scientific observer who summarizes a situation necessarily distinguishes between the structure of expectations with which a given policy is inaugurated and the expectations that prevail when there are opportunities to put it into effect.

Our conception does not regard as power all effects that follow from what X does in relation to Y. A price policy set by a corporation influences the real standard of living of those who buy or sell the product, and contributes to the level of employment and production throughout the economy. These reverberations are part of the total influence of X on human relations, as implemented by the setting of a price. Power enters into the picture when the price is flouted by those expected by the corporation to adhere to it, followed by the imposing of deprivations upon them. If another firm does not follow the new line and begins to undercut, X may drive Y out of business by engaging in a price war until Y is financially exhausted; or by conniving with shippers to mishandle Y's product; or by threatening to withhold desired goods from jobbers, wholesalers and retailers who use Y's goods . . . and so on through a long list of available means of inflicting a deprivation. Observe that X may be aware that the firm has no legal or moral authority to expect Y to follow the price lead, or to punish Y for refusing to do so. (And perhaps Y is able to falsify the expectations of X by invoking the courts to intervene against unfair business practice.)

This example shows that while power does not necessarily coincide with the domain of influence exerted by a given action, *any human situation can be converted into a power relation*. This can be done if a participant demands certain conduct and "thinks he can get away with it" by threatening or actually inflicting severe deprivations on anyone who deviates. But the transformation is not complete unless others validate the expectation by conforming to the pattern prescribed. Without closing this circle of passive acquiescence or active consent the power relation would not be complete.

We speak of the *politicizing* of human relations when they are transformed into power relationships. The ultimate is a totalitarian state that has swallowed up all of society by prescribing a norm for every detail of conduct and subjecting it to sanction. Prisons are the final expression of this process, and the prison state, a variant of the garrison state in which the military dominate, is the form taken by some totalitarian regimes. (15)

THE SOCIAL PROCESS

That men want power is a statement we can accept as true in every society where power exists; and this is not to say whether everybody wants it with the same intensity, or whether the drive for power is innate or acquired. For the purpose of analyzing the social process, power is unmistakably a value, in the sense that it is desired (or likely to be desired). Participation in the making of decisions (power) is a value; access to goods and services (wealth) is a value. Since we are interested in the interrelations of power with personality and the whole social process, it is perhaps useful to provide a succinct outline of the process. In the social process:

> *Man*
> pursues *Values*
> through *Institutions*
> on *Resources*. (16)

Power and *wealth* we have already mentioned. *Wellbeing*, in the sense of bodily and psychic integrity, is a value. *Enlightenment* is the finding and spreading of knowledge. There is *skill*, the acquiring and using of dexterities. *Respect* covers what is often called social class position. *Affection* includes friendship and also sexual intimacy. *Rectitude* is the value of morality. This is a representative, not an exhaustive, list of values. It is not a ranking of values in order of importance in American or any other culture. We assume that the relative position of values varies from group to group, from person to person and from time to time in the history of any culture or personality.

Values are shaped and shared in patterns that we call *institutions*. The following table gives a hint of the relation between the values we have named and the institutions usually specialized to each in our civilization:

VALUE	INSTITUTION
Power	Government
Respect	Social class distinctions
Affection	Family, friendship, intimacy
Rectitude	Church, home
Well-being	Hospital, clinic
Wealth	Business
Enlightenment	Research, education, information
Skill	Occupations (17)

Although it is correct to say that patterns of activity are usually specialized to the shaping and sharing of specific values, detailed analysis of a situation always reveals that any given practice is included among the institutions of more than one value. A legislative session, for instance, is concerned with *power* in the voting of bills, with *respect* in the social class distinctions adhered to among members, *affection* in the intimacies that develop, *rectitude* in the invocation of standards of right and wrong, *well-being* in the possible sharing of infectious diseases, *wealth* in the payment of members, *enlightenment* in the hearing of testimony, *skill* in the perfection of oratorical and other techniques.

The degree to which X influences a decision measures the weight of the power of X. The domain of power is the people affected by it. The range is the list of values affected by the decision (a legislature, for instance, can regulate wealth and many other values). The scope of power is the degree to which the individual range values are influenced. We may also speak of base values when we refer to the use of values to affect one another. Hence power can be a base for wealth, and wealth a base for power.

Such, then, is the general analysis of power, which we describe as a special kind of policy making. When the policies are expected to be enforced against an obstructor by the imposing of extreme deprivations, we have decision, which is a power relation. The offender can be deprived of any or all values. Perhaps it is power (i.e., removal from office). It may be respect (loss of social class privileges). It may be affection (forbidding of friendly association). It may be rectitude (excoriation). It may be well-being (mutilation). Perhaps it is wealth (fines). Possibly enlightenment (exclusion from access to information) or skill (prohibition of exercise).

Power conceived as decision is more useful for political science than Bertrand Russell's definition of power as "the production of intended effects." (18) Since we are concerned with conduct, we are not interested in all effects, including effects on nature (save as they affect conduct). "Intended effects on conduct" is also too broad, covering as it does every successful exercise of manipulative ability.

In this book we are not concerned with the power process as a whole, but rather with the interplay of power and personality. As the man in the street puts it: Are there "born leaders" and "born followers"? As a specialist might phrase it: Are there early experiences in childhood and youth which, impinging upon a basic biological type, culminate in personalities oriented toward power? Is there, in a word, a political man, a *homo politicus,* a basic political type? It is our purpose to determine whether recent advances in the social, psychological and medical sciences have brought us any nearer than our ancestors to an intelligent understanding of the interaction of personality and power. If so, we can make recommendations with more confidence regarding the development of an elite appropriate to the needs of a society that aspires toward freedom.

II. POLITICAL ROLE
AND POLITICAL TYPE

THE QUESTION of basic type rises from the common observation that men can have power without wanting it, or want power without having it. The playing of a role in politics, therefore, does not have the same meaning to different persons. The conception of a political type is that some personalities are power seekers, searching out the power institutions of the society into which they are born and devoting themselves to the capture and use of government.

The most convincing evidence that some men do not attach overwhelming importance to power is that, though born into high position, they voluntarily give up their place for "the woman I love," or for religious meditation, scholarly work or some other activity. Some men have risen to great heights and laid power down after having exercised it fully. Such a one is the Cincinnatus of tradition, called from his field to assume the dictatorship, yet remaining eager to return to the plow.

One of the most obliging figures among those unconcerned with power was Ramiro, the brother of Alfonso I of Aragon, chosen to succeed the king in 1134. Ramiro was a monk who came out of his retirement long enough to marry and achieve a daughter whom he promptly married to the ruler of Catalonia. Leaving the child under the guardianship of her husband, Ramiro happily returned to the monastery within three years with the succession satisfactorily settled.

In striking contrast are the power holders who cling to power to the point of provoking assassination; or the power holders who have committed suicide when turned out of office, although in no danger of death, disgrace or impoverishment. Milder examples are senators and judges who have stayed in office long after their intellectual and physical strength has failed, at no little loss of respect; and officials who, on failing of reappointment or re-election, have succumbed to some depression or illness traceable to their exclusion from office.

There is no doubt that the inner orientation toward power is a significant factor in politics, a factor to be taken into account in any scientific or practical consideration of public affairs. We are often told, for example, that persons who are wholly absorbed in getting and holding power to the exclusion of other values are dangerous members of society. On the other hand, we are warned that lack of interest in power abandons society to the egocentric exploiters of human frailty. If either hypothesis is correct—and there is much to lend plausibility to both—we are dealing with a dynamic factor in society that needs to be thoroughly understood and controlled in the interest of our basic goal-values.

The notion of a political type is that of a developmental type who passes through a distinctive career line in which the power opportunities of each situation are selected in preference to other opportunities. As such a person moves from infancy through maturity, he becomes progressively predisposed to respond to the power-shaping and power-sharing possibilities of each situation in which he finds himself.

If there is a political type in this sense, the basic characteristic will be the *accentuation of power in relation to other values within the personality when compared with other persons.*

Besides the basic political type, we are interested in the possibility of discovering the special development that sets up an inner demand to play one political role rather than another. Some political specializations are limited to the exercise of a single major skill, while others involve an exceedingly complex pattern. Some political careers are based upon the control of a single value; others are more diversified. And some political roles use power as a base for more power, or subordinate power to a variety of other ends.

POLITICAL SPECIALIZATIONS

Before we attempt to unify the theory of general or special political types, let us remind ourselves of the enormous range and variety of roles that must be taken into account. Even a cursory survey of those who have played historically prominent roles in politics discloses an almost overwhelming diversity.

Any panorama of political roles brings into relief the empire builders, the men who have brought into a single political edifice peoples of many contrasting cultures. Such empire builders are Genghis Khan, Alexander, Cyrus and Hammurabi.

There are restorers of order after a "time of trouble" in which political unity has split into fragments, and great states are torn by dissension and war. The founder of nearly every dynasty in China was such a restorer, welding together the remnants of an imperial organization. After a long period of disorder the Sui and the T'ang dynasties, for instance, brought unity under Yang Chien and Li Yuan (and his son, Li Shih-min). When the T'ang faded and crumbled, the Sung came into being with Chao K'uang-yin. In the history of the Roman Empire, Diocletian was such a restorer in the West, Constantine in the East.

Our analysis must take into account political leaders who have set up effective monarchies by subordinating to the Crown the feudal or ecclesiastical authorities who previously wielded formal or effective power. In England, Henry VIII was such a leader, typical of the many states in which political development at one time pivoted around a national king.

We need to consider the founders of national independence, the "fathers" of their country, like Washington who led the American colonists in the war of secession from Britain and in the eventual consolidation of "a more perfect union." Masaryk is an example of a statesman-civilian who liberated his people.

The panorama of political leaders includes also men who, like Lincoln, have been consolidators of nation-states which were passing through acute periods of civil strife.

And there are sociopolitical revolutionaries who have fought to enlarge the basis of political and social participation. A few have been successful, like Lenin; others, like Spartacus, leader of the gladiatorial insurrection at Rome, have quickly succumbed to defeat. In this category come the modernizers of countries that have lagged behind the technological development of the rest of the world (Kamal Atatürk in Turkey; the modernizers of Japan).

Many sociopolitical revolutionists fought against the broadening of participation in political and other values.

The Mediterranean world of classical days often witnessed antidemocratic oligarchies and tyrannies established on the ruins of popular governments in city states. And in recent years we have witnessed in large-scale states, like Germany and Italy, the meteoric rise of antidemocratic leaders of the stamp of Hitler, Mussolini and their facsimiles.

Many leaders have combined facility in agitation, strategy, diplomacy and other tools of power in their own hands. However, the gallery of famous political personages takes in many specialists who have excelled in the performance of a single role.

Savonarola was an agitational flame, capable of whipping popular passion to the peak. He was the persecutory type of agitator, not the enthusiast. Savonarola relied upon invective as a principal weapon, unlike some of the nineteenth-century utopians, such as Albert Brisbane, who "accentuated the positive" in seeking support for social reconstruction. Agitators are specialized according to their favorite instrument of communication. Unlike Savonarola, who was a man of the tongue, Jefferson was a wielder of the pen, and found it next to impossible to speak in public.

Special forms of advocacy develop in the arenas furnished by various political institutions. In connection with the Roman Senate we remember Cicero. British parliamentary life has given rise to the adroit managerial technique of Walpole and Palmerston, the eloquence of Chatham, the debating skill of Fox and the impressive substance of Burke.

We cannot overlook the judge-legislator-arbitrator, the roles performed by men chosen by their fellows to make an end to disputes. Solon is the prototype, having been accepted by all parties in Athens, despite his middle-class connections, to institute reforms. (He was made sole archon in 594 B.C. to remedy the distress caused by the introduction of coined money and the resulting high rates of interest.)

Some careers rest on original ideas about the long-range objectives of policy and the expedients appropriate to their attainment. Jeremy Bentham, for instance, was a true inventor and planner.

Although the advisory role may include the thinking up of new ways of doing things, the core of the adviser's function is the critical evaluation of the alternatives put before him.

Because of the overwhelming importance of the future for policy, rulers have sought the aid of all who promised to divine the shape of things to come, and tried to suppress forecasters or predictors inimical to their power. During the reign of Charlemagne's successor, Louis the Pious, we are told that the great lords possessed their own astrologers. The emperors of Rome occasionally banished the astrologers—except their own—from Rome or Italy because they had been too bold in predicting the death of the emperor. Today the statistical chart takes the place of magician (and most of the astrologers).

Some of the most illustrious among those who specialize in philosophy or science (enlightenment) have been theorists who have built up systematic justifications of some pattern of power. Bodin devised a theory of sovereignty that was a potent doctrine in the struggle of national monarchs for a place in the sun. Systematic code makers, like Calvin, have contributed a political formula as well as a doctrine by giving authoritative shape to the detailed structure of government. In contrast with systematic specialists on normative standards, some intellectuals have been more devoted to systematic observation and explanation (science), after the pattern of Aristotle in the *Politics*. Many writers are impressionistic (or perhaps one should say, artistic) rather than systematic, whether their preoccupation is with normative or descriptive problems.

No inventory of political roles, however abbreviated, can refrain from taking note of the diplomat, whose specialty, of course, is negotiation (Metternich, Talleyrand). Usually the term is limited to designating official representatives of a ruler in foreign affairs, but the basic function goes on incessantly in internal politics, where deals are perpetually under negotiation. We have no comprehensive term for the specialty in both arenas, since the word "bargainer" or "trader" has been pre-empted for the market. The function has many subdivisions, including the fixer, who acts on the basis of a reputation for influence with the powerful and engages in the making of arrangements that, if exposed to public view, would arouse general indignation.

When we speak of official, party, pressure-group or other organizations we quickly note the administrator, who looks after the continuous operation of the undertaking within a framework of authority and control. Among the famous administrators of history was Wang An-shih who in eleventh-century China remained in power for several years and put through a series of striking reforms. In recent times we have seen how the party specialist on administration may maneuver himself into a decisive position and outreach spectacular figures who excel in agitation and theory. I refer to Stalin, winner of the duel with Trotsky.

The specialization may not be primarily on symbols (theorists, agitators) or procedures of administration, but upon the use of the instrumentalities of violence. Here are included the military and police (not to forget the political policemen and spies like Fouché of Napoleon's time, or Asef, the Czarist spy).

THE BASES OF POWER

If we look into the bases on which power has been attained, whatever the role, the theme of diversity is amply supported. Power may be based on power, as when it depends on being born to a privileged position.

More striking are the careers founded almost exclusively upon such physical characteristics as large stature, energy and co-ordination. Verus Maximinus would never have been heard of save for his huge size, which so impressed the legions on the Rhine that they proclaimed this untutored Thracian peasant emperor. In small groups or in turbulent times (when the expectation of violence is present) the comparatively rudimentary fact of physical strength is no mean advantage. At all times unusual capacity for work, and especially for concentration, is an asset. Gladstone was notable for his ability to concentrate for long hours, thoroughly covering an enormous amount of ground. And Justinian I of the sixth-century Roman Empire in the East is only one of a number of leaders who have possessed extraordinary ability to go without food and sleep. *Wellbeing*, then, is sometimes a decisive base value for the acquisition of power.

Or the principal base may be *wealth*. The interplay is illustrated by the history of Crassus who used his power to increase his wealth in order, in turn, to expand his power. As a favorite of Sulla he had become an exceedingly wealthy man by buying up the property of proscribed Roman citizens. In our own society the role of wealth as a steppingstone to power is only too well known.

Knowledge (*enlightenment*) is the asset upon which power is often based, although there is a notable dearth of historical examples of outstanding philosophers or scholars who have risen to the very pinnacle of power. Indeed, much is made of the fact that Confucius failed to secure the co-operation of his prince when he served as minister of justice in the state of Lu for four brief years, and that Plato, called in by the uncle of the tyrant of Syracuse, was successful neither in educating the nephew nor in moderating the failings of the uncle. Often a philosopher or scholar comes in touch with a ruler in the capacity of tutor; Louis XV of France was acting in no unusual way when he appointed his former tutor as chief minister.

Proficiency in almost any *skill* can provide a springboard for personal contact or general celebrity, and thence lead to power. Paderewski's wizardry at the keyboard was a factor in numbering him among the leaders of a liberated Poland. Scientific knowledge was an element in the career of de Valera among his compatriots in Eire, and of Weitzmann among the Zionists.

Power may also be based on social position (*respect*). The impact of an upper-class family name has so frequently played a decisive part in the lives of public men that it would be more than usually invidious to name an example. Sometimes, of course, a lowly respect position is the asset (remember the "log cabin" tradition in the U.S., and the virtue of "proletarian" origin in the U.S.S.R.).

The base value may be *affection,* whether in the form of friendship or sexual love. (Sexual attractiveness may be closely associated, but is not invariably correlated, with the physical qualities referred to above as well-being.) The role of sex as a means to power has been brought to public notice on many dramatic occasions, especially when a powerful person has become infatuated with an "unsuitable" person, but has overridden these objections and launched his favorite on an influential career. The Empress Theodora of the Byzantine Empire, we are told, was a courtesan before her marriage. One of the three husbands of the Empress Zoë, daughter of Constantine, is said to have been of lowly origin. Likewise, homosexual attractiveness is at the basis of the career of some men and women.

It is notorious that intermarriage among ruling families may involve little sexual or friendly interest on the part of the participants. Intermarriage often operates as a hostage system for the performance of an agreement, and is then an example of power rather than affection. The "marrying Habsburgs" are famous; and it is not untypical that in the struggle for power in Rome among the triumvirs, intermarriages figured. Caesar's daughter Julia was married to Pompey, and her death was a contributing factor to the estrangement with Caesar. After the death of Julia, Pompey married the widow of Crassus. Antony married Octavian's sister Octavia, and later his open association with Cleopatra was a factor in breaking up the second triumvirate.

In many cases uprightness (a reputation for *rectitude*) is a basis of power. A vital step in many political careers has been the reputation for moral integrity resulting from the open championship of unpopular causes. John Adams and Josiah Quincy, Jr., for instance, put their legal services at the disposal of the British soldiers who were arrested after the "Boston massacre." And it has been remarked that many British public men have stood out against dominant public opinion and sentiment at early stages of their careers. On the other hand, there are careers that have been furthered by a reputation for unscrupulousness which has led to their being selected in order to meet an emergency in which men bound to older conceptions of decency were handicapped.

In innumerable instances the possibility of using a base

value in the climb toward power has depended upon "luck" in the simple sense of an episode beyond ordinary expectations. We are told that Cranmer's great opportunity came when "by chance" his argument showing how Henry VIII could divorce his wife without appealing to Rome came to the notice of the king. Presently Cranmer was archbishop.

POWER AS A BASE VALUE

The diversity of political careers is emphasized anew when we look into the use of power as a base for the acquisition of more power, or of other values.

The Emperor Shien Tsung of China (A.D. 806–820) was in terror of disease and death, and determined to live forever. He surrounded himself with persons alleged to have a means of curing or preventing disease and of refilling the fountain of youth. The emperor used all his power to the fullest extent possible in the pursuit of *well-being,* in the sense of physical and psychic integrity. Unhappily he (and his son) died from overdoses of the elixir of perpetual life.

That the instruments of power can be subordinated to the accumulation of wealth is common observation, especially in the case of city machine bosses who use politics to get contracts or payment for favors. Historians have painted Louis XI of France as a fifteenth-century monarch exceedingly captivated by the possibilities of using power and wealth in a never-ceasing spiral. He ruled like a modern capitalist, placing bribes like investments in the courts of his enemies and dreaming of a great trading company to monopolize the Mediterranean.

Occasionally the resources of power have been taken advantage of for the purpose of adding to the knowledge (enlightenment) of the power holder. Michael VII, eleventh-century emperor of the Byzantine Empire, devoted himself almost entirely to scholarly pursuits, relying especially upon the famous scholar of the day, Michael Psellus.

Some power holders have occupied themselves with the acquisition of skills, resembling what Otto Fenichel called a "Don Juan of Achievement." Emperor Frederick II made of his thirteenth-century Sicilian court a center of cultural activity. He learned six languages and experimented in many types of literary and bodily pursuits. He was a competent soldier and diplomat, and both licentious and luxurious in his intimate life. The emperor wrote a serious treatise on falconry, and shaped a law code that was the most elaborate in Europe after Charlemagne.

Power is often utilized with an eye to respect even more than to power. This is conspicuous when someone of humble respect position gains great power and proceeds to glorify himself and his family. Obviously this can aid in perpetuating and expanding power, but it is also possible to consolidate and extend power without relying quite so heavily upon moves designed to arouse continuous expressions of admiration. The Emperor Vespasian was the son of a humble tax collector from the Italian municipality of Reate and took seriously the task of bringing himself to a level with his aristocratic Roman predecessors. He began the Coliseum and arranged for his son Titus to have one of the most elaborate triumphs ever seen in Rome. Vespasian also began the restoration of the capitol.

The use of power as a means of affection has aroused the romantic exaggerations so characteristic of personalized history. Everyone is aware of the fabulous prowess of Messalina and of Catherine II.

Power can be subordinated to considerations of rectitude, in the sense that a major if not a leading preoccupation of the power holder is with ethics and religion. One of the most sensational examples is Ikhnaton (Amenho-tep IV of Egypt), who became wholly absorbed in in-augurating the worship of the Sun-god Aton and achieved a universal conception beautifully formulated in hymns of enduring worth. As James H. Breasted has emphasized, it is astonishing to learn that the arrangement of subject matter in these poems is identical with part of the psalms in the Old Testament, which are many centuries later.

There are many examples of power seekers and holders who have integrated their power with the successful pursuit of many values and have lived remarkably full lives. Louis IX of thirteenth-century France was undoubtedly such a figure. He was taller by a head than any of his knights and excelled in the physical arts of war and peace. Saint Louis lived according to the strenuous conceptions of recti-tude current in the Middle Ages. We know that he fasted much, listened attentively to sermons, regularly heard two masses a day and all the offices (actually dressing at mid-night for matins in his chapel). When he traveled, Louis surrounded himself with priests on horseback who chanted the hours. He went on two crusades, visited hospitals, tended the sick himself and gave abundant charity to beg-gars every day. And his courtly display set a new standard of opulence for France. Louis was his own prime minister. We are told that, though "naturally cold" in temperament, he possessed a marked sense of humor and no little wit.

CULTURE PATTERN AND POLITICAL TYPE

After reminding ourselves of the great variety of political roles, we come back to the central question: Despite all this diversity is there a political type, a personality in which power is accentuated?

We note first the importance of recognizing what **is**

meant by the *accentuation* of power. Accentuation is a conception of cultural relativity, and it implies that the political type developed in one setting may attach very different importance to power from that given to it by the political type elsewhere. Power can be accentuated in relation to other values and to other people and still occupy a rather low rank among values. Cultures rank values in different ways, and every personality exposed to the pattern of a culture tends to take over the same rank order. Within this system of ranking, there is room for over- or under-emphasis; and relative stress on power is what we mean by its accentuation. (1)

The rank order of power in relation to other values is high in some cultures, and anyone who accentuates power in such a setting closely approximates the most drastic popular and scientific idea of what constitutes the *homo politicus*. There is no doubt that the warrior was a high-ranking type in the culture into which Genghis Khan was born. (2) But in some societies leadership whether in war or peace is rated lower than participation in other values. For instance, the possession of a religious dance entitling one to a respected place in tribal ceremonies may be more important than power or wealth. This is reported to be true of at least some of the Indians of southwestern United States.

On the other hand, we know of cultures (or historical situations within a broad culture area) in which wealth predominates. As Miriam Beard has pointed out, there have been two flowerings of business states in the history of the Mediterranean world. (3) The first began around 1000 B.C. and came to a climax around 500 B.C., the second beginning around A.D. 1000 and blooming about A.D. 1500. Both were epochs of commercial cities run by oligarchies based on wealth and using power to maintain and enhance wealth. The great trading cities of Asia Minor and the Greek colonies in southern Italy and Sicily were prominent in the earlier period. The Lydians built Sardis. The Ionian Greeks had Miletus, Rhodes and other flourishing centers. And there was Corinth; and the Phoenician Tyre, Sidon and Carthage. In northern Italy were the Etruscan cities. The second epoch was created by Lübeck and the other towns of the Hanseatic League in northern Europe and by the Italian merchants of Venice, Florence and other commercial communities. The business-city states of the first period gradually gave way to the Roman Empire; the states of the later period were cut short by the rise of national monarchies.

Rich men typically monopolized the governing jobs, as in Carthage where, as Aristotle pointed out, officials were allowed to continue in gainful occupations which Roman senators were supposed to avoid. Perhaps three hundred wealthy families ran Carthage. Similarly, the rich families of Venice held a tight monopoly of governing positions. Approximately 1,000 men and their families, having incomes ranging from 200,000 to 500,000 lire a year, formed the elite of a population of 190,000. In Florence the rich families did not succeed in getting a stranglehold on power but had to keep continually on the alert in a perpetual struggle between the upper classes, who were called the *popolo grasso* or fat people, and the small or lean folk, who were known as the *popolo minuto*. The situation put more stress on power and nurtured such figures as the Medicis.

SOCIAL STRUCTURE AND POLITICAL TYPE

In gauging the degree to which any person has accentuated power, it is appropriate to examine his position at birth in the social structure and to take note of the political expectancy of those born into that stratum. An analysis of the British House of Commons which included all parliaments from 1918 through 1935 showed that families with hereditary titles, for instance, had at least four hundred times the representation they would have received on a proportionate basis. (4) Comparing the average House of Commons with the general population, it appears that the "domestic workers" are practically unrepresented and that the "rank-and-file workers" have little more than one-third of their proportionate share of the membership. Employers, managers and professional workers, on the other hand, were relatively overrepresented (the professional workers having more than twelve times as many members as their respective numbers would warrant).

Further indication of the relation between social class (respect class) and politics in Britain comes from an analysis made by Harold J. Laski of the 306 persons who held Cabinet offices between 1801 and 1924. (5) Nearly 60 per cent of the ministers were born of immediately aristocratic parentage (and nearly 80 per cent were either at Oxford or Cambridge). Only 30 per cent were dependent upon their own efforts for a livelihood, and of these nearly one-half were lawyers. The aristocracy from which the Cabinet members were drawn consisted of a thousand families; but the actual number of families from which Cabinet ministers were drawn was much smaller. The Cecil family and its relatives contributed six, the Greys five, the Stanleys four. Taking the period as a whole, the decline of aristocracy was gradual (even including the first labor government).

Although the legislature and the upper reaches of the executive remained resistant to a broadened basis of recruitment, the administrative services were overrun. By the first decade of the present century the higher administrative posts had become the special preserve of the upper middle classes and in the Class I examination of 1911, the sons of merchants were more successful than those of any other occupational category, while the parents of but 2 per cent of the successful candidates were classed as "landed proprietor" or "of no occupation." This may be contrasted with the situation in the years 1836–54 when the Treasury appointed twenty-two clerks direct from school to the General Registry Office. Only one was the son of a merchant, and the fathers of more than 70 per cent were either officials or landed proprietors. (6)

Prediction tables could be worked out for every position in a given society, and the notion of the accentuation of politics can therefore be expressed in rather precise terms. In a caste society the entire career line is rigidly limited to certain conventional trajectories. As societies gain in social mobility, the amount of rising and falling increases. But even within the highly stratified, closed class societies, there is opportunity for the accentuation of politics when a person becomes more intensely devoted to the pursuit of power than is customary.

SOCIAL CRISIS AND POLITICAL TYPE

Standard expectancies are a function not only of position in the social structure but also of the intensity and type of social crisis. The relation of wealth to government in the United States has undergone long-term changes. In colonial days the wealthy merchants and landholders personally participated in office holding in the government. After the democratization of the franchise, and concurrently with the colossal expansion of American economic life, the wealthiest men withdrew from direct office holding and resorted to indirect means of control, such as the financing of professional politicians, political parties and pressure groups. By 1855, for instance, in the state of New York, the richest men held no office. One investigator found 29 millionaires, no one of whom held an office. Of the 118 who were rated between $500,000 and $1,000,000, only one was found. It is noteworthy, however, that during periods of internal crisis, like the Civil War, or of external crisis, like our major wars, the members of wealthy families have tended to engage directly in government in elective and appointive offices. (7)

Political expectancy tables can be constructed for many other characteristics than position of family in the prevailing value-structure under various degrees of crisis. Regional position is no insignificant factor. In communities where business opportunities are comparatively few, party and governmental activity is stimulated by the relative advantages of getting and controlling the perquisites of office. This is true of some of our thinly populated and industrially underdeveloped states. In the impoverished South, politics and the armed forces offered great opportunities to the young white southerner.

Predictions can be made of the political expectancy of groups selected by sex, age, physique and other biological criteria of direct or indirect social importance. (8)

THE POLITICAL TYPE

We now turn directly to the general theory of political personality. Power is accentuated in personalities under certain conditions of motivation, skill and opportunity. Yearning for power is not enough. It is essential to acquire and exercise appropriate skill with at least a minimum degree of effectiveness. We do not include among the fully developed political personalities those individuals who stay on the sidelines swathed in delusions of public grandeur. Our conception also excludes persons possessing power, yet attaching little importance to it (in comparison with the value-scale of other power holders).

The political type is characterized by an intense and ungratified craving for deference.

These cravings, both accentuated and unsatisfied in the primary circle, are displaced upon public objects (persons and practices connected with the power process).

The displacement is rationalized in terms of public interest.

We sum up the political type in terms of the development of motive as follows:

> Private Motives
> Displaced on Public Objects
> Rationalized in Terms of Public Interest. (9)

So far as skill is concerned, the principal asset is what Charles E. Merriam called "facility in group combination," which means the selection of procedures by which favorable power balances are attained. A favorable balance is achieved by retaining crystallized support, and by winning over or neutralizing the indifferent and hostile.

III. THE POLITICAL
PERSONALITY

POWER AS COMPENSATION

OUR KEY hypothesis about the power seeker is that he pursues power as a means of compensation against deprivation. *Power is expected to overcome low estimates of the self,* by changing either the traits of the self or the environment in which it functions.

The self typically includes more than the primary ego, which is the symbol used by a person to refer to his irreducible "I," "me." (1) The self takes in whatever is included with the primary ego as belonging with it. The boundaries of the self ordinarily include—besides the primary ego symbols—symbols that refer to parents, wife, children, friends, countrymen, coreligionists and other groups and individuals. These are the symbols of identification.

The personality includes demands made *by* the self *on* the primary egó and on each constituent part of the self. Everyone makes demands on every member of a group with which he is identified, including himself.

Besides identifications and demands, there are expectations about the self in relation to the world. The primary ego or the constituent elements are deprived to the extent that they do not enjoy the value position demanded, whether the value in question is well-being or any other in the list we have been using for descriptive purposes. Furthermore, the self is regarded as deprived when it is moving into a future in which loss of value position is held likely, or failure to overcome obstacles in the way of expanding values is foreseen. (Deprivations are endured or threatened losses, and endured or threatened obstructions to an improved value position.)

Our hypothesis about the power-accentuating type is that power is resorted to when it is expected to contribute more than any alternative value to overcoming or obviating deprivations of the self. (2) The deprivations may be appraised in terms of any value, and any component of the self-structure may be involved.

WHEN COMPENSATION OCCURS

Deprivations may be met not by compensatory strivings but by withdrawal from active participation in human relationships. What are the conditions favoring compensation rather than acquiescence?

One set of conditions is related to the deprivation: *compensation is favored when the deprivation is not overwhelming.* For if the blows of fortune are too hard to bear, the individual and the group may withdraw from the arena of power. The individual may commit suicide, even when not threatened by retaliation; and the group may abandon its own institutions, either taking over the culture of another or physically disappearing. (3)

Deprivations are not regarded as overwhelming *when lost or denied indulgences are not demanded absolutely.* The man who kills himself when he is rejected at the polls has made an absolutely rigid demand upon himself; this *or else.*

Deprivations are not regarded as overwhelming *when they are not wholly attributed to the self*. If it is possible to absolve the self from responsibility by blaming superior forces at the disposal of an enemy, or immoral conduct on the part of the antagonist, the demand on the self is sufficiently flexible to permit life to go on.

It is also true that deprivations can be better borne when they are *accompanied by some indulgences*. The man who fights a good fight can sometimes save his self-respect when he loses power or wealth. Losses can sometimes be minimized, as when they are less than expected.

A second set of conditions is favorable to compensation; *compensation by the use of power is facilitated when it is expected to yield more net values than can be obtained by the use of other alternatives.*

Favorable expectations about power occur among those who have *successfully used power* in the past under similar circumstances, or who know of such use by others. Professional soldiers are often more calm in military disaster than civilians who imagine "all is lost." Seasoned party politicians are famous for the cold-bloodedness with which they can survive defeat.

INDOCTRINATION WITH A MISSION

The conception of political type that has just been outlined is put forward as a means of unifying the data of history, social science, psychology and medicine. It appears to be confirmed by what we know of many of the outstanding figures in the history of political life, especially in the case of men who were indoctrinated from the earliest years with a political mission. In these instances all of our specifications are met. The individual was identified with the destiny of a group larger than his primary ego. The emphasis on mission rose from the discrepancy between the goals of the group and the present or prospective situation in which the group appeared to be. Group losses or obstructions, it was believed, could be removed by power (though not necessarily to the exclusion of other means). Moreover, power was glorified as a probable—if not inevitable—means of fulfilling the collective mission and hence of removing and preventing deprivation. The focus of attention of the developing youngster has been absorbed with symbols of reference to power and with rationalizations of power. Immediate indulgences have been granted to him as he acquired the skills deemed appropriate to the mission to be fulfilled. Such intense indoctrination usually occurs when a changing political situation is surcharged with conflict, or when checks and losses are fresh.

Recall the story of Hannibal, indoctrinated from childhood with burning hatred of Rome and loyalty to Carthage by his able father, the Carthaginian general Hamilcar Barcas. This occurred in the thick of the duel which ultimately led to the extinction of Carthage in the struggle for Mediterranean primacy between the two great super powers of the time. (4)

Gustavus Adolphus of Sweden was trained from the first by his austere parents (Charles IX and Christina) to be a champion of Protestantism. He learned Swedish and German as his mother tongues, and at twelve had mastered Latin, Italian and Dutch. Later he acquired a working knowledge of Spanish, Russian and Polish. The boy began to take a responsible place in public ceremonies during his ninth year. At thirteen he received petitions and conversed officially with foreign ministers. Two years later he administered a Duchy, and within a year was practically coregent. He was trained in martial and chivalric skills, and his subsequent record speaks for itself in the struggle against the Catholic powers.

The importance of ambitious and loving parents in shaping the ego ideal (the demands made on the self) is a commonplace of everyday wisdom and scientific observation. Although we know little of the details of the early life of Genghis Khan, everything points to the decisive influence of his mother in preparing him to restore the position of the family. It was a period in which the great clans were giving way to smaller social units, the family. Families with large herds of horses were able to support a large following of armed riders as well as slaves to do the menial work of the camp. Weaker families were compelled to get on as best they could outside the lands of the aristocrats. Temujin (later Genghis Khan) was born into a broken-down family of Mongols with memories of a heroic past but surrounded by present adversity. Temujin's father was poisoned by enemies before the boy went on his first hunt. Temujin and his brothers hunted marmots and mice, and they even caught fish in the streams, which no self-respecting Mongol was supposed to eat. The mother kept them alive and did what she could to inspire them with the pride and self-confidence that came from the heroic legends of past greatness. She tried to keep together the small band that had still clustered around her husband. In the rough and tumble of the steppes, Genghis formed his whole life in the struggle to survive, to overcome, to bend men to his will. As he once declared, "a man's highest job in life is to break his enemies, to drive them before him, to take from them all the things that have been theirs, to hear the weeping of those who cherished them, to take their horses between his knees, and to press in his arms the most desirable of their women."

This is typical of the burning ambition for restoration and revenge of those who have been deprived of the power to which they believed themselves entitled. And in fashioning the instrument of restoring the family fortunes, the role of the mother, as in the case of the great Khan, is often exemplified. A more humble instance is the life of Napoleon III, who was so profoundly shaped by his mother. Louis Bonaparte, his father, was a brother of Napoleon I and had been king of Holland. At one point in Louis's career, he had compelled his wife, by a "scandalous" legal action, to give up to him the elder of her two children. With Charles she wandered from Geneva to Aix, Carlsruhe to Augsburg, and supervised the son's education, whether he studied in a school or with tutors.

EXTREMES OF INDULGENCE AND DEPRIVATION

Our recent advances in studying personality development have given us greater understanding of the process by which extreme cravings for power, respect and related deference values come into existence and find outlet in positive forms of activity, rather than in total withdrawal. An essential factor is the balancing of deprivation by indulgence; and, more particularly, the tensions arising from extremes of both. Without a compensating flow of affection and admiration, deprivations may appear too overwhelming to justify the exertions necessary to acquire the skills essential to eventual success. And if the flow swings erratically from extreme to extreme, the tensions of uncertainty can be kept within bearable limits, so that energies are concentrated upon the task of mastering the environment.

We know that one of the tension-inducing environments is created when affection, respect and other values are (or are felt to be) contingent upon the acquisition and exercise

of skills. To some degree, of course, this process is inseparable from the early contact of the infant and child with the
standards imposed upon him by the carriers of the culture
into which he is born. Unless some obedience is given, there
is punishment in the form of bodily chastisement, withdrawal of affection and other deprivations. With conform-
ity, on the other hand, rewards are forthcoming in the
form of food, affection and other indulgences. It is a question, here, not of this process in general but of the special
form given to it when the young person is exposed to a
relatively elaborate set of requirements, which are rewarded
or punished with special intensity. Almost all learning of
set tasks gives rise to characteristic deprivations. One must
practice grammar, for instance, at a set time whether one is
in the mood or not. The inhibiting of impulses to run and
play or to study something else often carries with it rage
reactions, reactions which may never rise to full expression in what is said and done or even thought. But these
answers to a command, whether emanating from outside
or from the internalized commander (the conscience), characteristically arouse tendencies to get out of the situation,
either by escape or by destruction. Such tendencies, if not
deliberately recognized and rejected, may give rise to a recurring level of tension against which defensive measures
are spontaneously taken. One of these measures is a blind
urge to act with intensity and rigidity; in short, the dynamisms of compulsiveness. The primary ego, caught in the
tug of conflicting impulses and requirements, can develop
a very extreme set of expectations about the characteristics
of the ego: on the one hand, the ego may appear to be loving and admired; on the other, the same ego can appear as
unloved, shameful, guilty and weak. Pessimism may rest
on the idea that one is loved only "conditionally"; that is,

that love can only be received as part of a bargain or a battle.

Certain eminent historical figures were subjected to great extremes of indulgence and deprivation, and they responded to the tension by great, even though reluctant, concentration upon power. Frederick the Great is a conspicuous example. His father, Frederick William I of Prussia, was reacting against the "French" standards that he thought had too much influenced his own father. Hence Frederick William imposed a regime of Spartan rigor on his son, hoping to make him a model soldier and a man of "thrift and frugality" after his own pattern. But the young Frederick sought and found indulgence in other pursuits. Encouraged by his mother and his governess, Madame de Roucouille, and his first tutor, Duhan, a French refugee, Frederick acquired a taste for music and literature, secretly learned Latin, which had been forbidden by his father, scoffed at religion, refused to ride or shoot and affected the French language, dress and manners, while deriding German uncouthness. Revolting against the harsh treatment received from his father, Frederick planned to run away to the English. But the secret was betrayed, with well-known results. One of the conspirators, Frederick's friend Katte, was beheaded in his presence. Eventually the crown prince began to conform as a means of obtaining power.

The impact of exposure to extreme indulgence and deprivation during formative years is exemplified further in such a career as that of Peter the Great. He saw one of his uncles dragged from the palace and butchered by a mob in 1682. He witnessed his mother's mentor and own best friend torn from his grasp and hacked to pieces in his presence. Exposed to the contempt of the boyars, and knowing of the contempt in which Russia was held abroad, Peter groped toward a career devoted to the internal consolidation of the Crown and the laying of the foundation for Russian power and fame abroad.

An interesting test case is Alexander the Great. Although we cannot completely penetrate the cloud of glorification with which his career is veiled, several strong indications can be found. His father, Philip of Macedon, was a strong and successful king in the very process of enlarging and consolidating his domain, taking advantage of the shifting constellation of power throughout the known world. In the full stride of conflict, he did not underrate the importance of having a successor properly equipped to deal with his new and heavy responsibilities. Alexander was not only given distinguished tutors, like Aristotle, but from early times he was subjected to a busy and by no means "soft" life. Of decisive significance, perhaps, was the soaring ambition of Alexander's mother, who was well acquainted with Eastern mystery cults, if not indeed a priestess before her marriage to Philip. How seriously Alexander took the tales of his divinity and his mission in the world, we cannot say. (When he gave encouragement to the belief in his divine attributes, he may have been deliberately employing a myth to consolidate his empire.)

We know that the devaluation of power among those born to power has been most conspicuous among those whose power is unchallenged, leaving them comparatively free to pursue other values.

When we consider less glamorous careers among those born to or claiming great power, the result is in harmony with our hypothetical picture of the political type. We know that middle-class homes are hothouses of ambition, holding their children to high standards of achievement, thus providing the tension between indulgence and deprivation so congenial to the accentuation of power. (5)

We know, too, that a disproportionately large contribution is made to the public service by professional families,
especially by clergymen and teachers. Many factors affect
this result. One element is exposure to a stream of talk
that typically contains many of the dominant rationalizations of public life. Facility in the use of words and familiarity with the history and traditions of public life are skills
that expedite the shaping of an active career in politics.
Contrast the articulateness of the clergyman or the teacher
with the inarticulateness of the typical manual toiler. The
symbols of reference to public targets and to plausible
means of rationalizing power foster the displacement of
private affects upon public objects. Middle-class professional families are the custodians of the dominant myths
of the community; and more. They emphasize the public
interest and glorify the professional standard of serving
collective rather than purely private advantage. This means
that business activity, for instance, is looked down upon,
however much the economic advantages of wealth are
openly or covertly desired. To be professional is to curb
the business standard of "charging what the traffic will
bear." The ideal is some form of direct public service, as
in law, medicine, education; and law, in particular, leads
to active participation in the power process.

Where crisis conditions prevail in modern society, the
educated and professional middle class has contributed
heavily to the leadership of political movements. Those
who sacrifice for the acquisition of any skill undergo self-
discipline; and they develop a moral claim on the world
for reward. Moreover, they are equipped with the symbols
most appropriate to the making of these claims plausible to
themselves and their fellows. When deprivations fall upon
them, they tend to respond with moral indignation. Not

only do they see that they are worse off; they believe it is unjust that they should be subject to deprivation. Hence it is easy for articulate professional families to rationalize their assertiveness in terms of the public good.

Furthermore, young people who have been reared in such an environment, even when they are unable or unwilling to acquire a long education, continue to apply strenuous standards to themselves. Whether they admit it or not, they feel acutely inferior when they fail to follow the accepted path. And their modes of compensation frequently take the form of what they conceive to be short cuts to the seizure of power and the regaining of a sense of total worth.

It is not to be forgotten that the tension between demands on the ego for both independence and dependence is intensified by a disciplinary-indulgent environment. This increases the likelihood of those vigorous compensations against dependency that enable many persons to impress upon others their seeming courage, intensity of conviction and strength of will. The child of our middle classes, for instance, is somewhat baffled by the intricate code that is forced upon him. On the one hand he is supposed to "be a nice boy" and not fight or engage in perversity, but on the other he is supposed to "stand up for himself" in altercations with other boys. And the niceties of the conduct appropriate to these commands are as intricate as the code of what is phrased as "selfishness" or "service." We laud business, yet deplore selfishness in the sense of outspoken pursuit of personal advantage. And our double standards create problems of adjustment that not infrequently are resolved by ruthless determination to escape from quandaries into action, and to use action as a means of silencing doubts by the fact and the fame of power.

"Mobility upward" along the power ladder is fostered by a home in which one member of the family, usually the mother, feels that she has married "beneath" her social (respect) class. These women are sensitive to the blight in their careers and obstinately determined to vindicate themselves by the vicarious triumphs of their children. Whether or not such ambitions are explicitly connected with the power myths and operations of society, they frequently create that taut internal state (that bifurcation of the ego into the secure and the insecure part) that favors the use of power as a way of relief.

A variant of the same compensatory response is the drive of the "provincial" or the "small-town boy" or the "country boy" to succeed against the stigma of rusticity. (6) One advantage of a marginal position in terms both of class structure and territory is that new power opportunities may be perceived and utilized free of older commitments. But the advantage from the side of motivation is the overcoming of a low-respect position through the use of power and other available means. Commentators have not failed to recognize that Napoleon came from the periphery of French power, Corsica, and that his family had long opposed the inclusion of the island in France. More recently the rise of Hitler and Rosenberg has emphasized certain advantages of a peripheral starting point.

That blighted careers make politicians is another observation in accord with our basic idea of the dynamic factors in leadership. A career is blighted when expectations are thwarted and when the responsibility can readily be projected from the self upon society. When power is the frustrator, restitution and retaliation in terms of power are plausible possibilities. The failure of the established order to put Doctor of Philosophy Marx in a Prussian university post was of no small consequence in launching him on his career. And this is not untypical of the response to be expected of men who have sacrificed to acquire a skill for which society provides no suitable scope. Hence the dynamic role so often noted of students and unemployed intellectuals in movements of political protest. (7)

The person who has not passed the preliminary qualifications expected for a recognized place in society is another potential recruit in the power struggle. Sometimes disturbed times or economic adversity has prevented the completion of a regular education. Or the person is rebellious against the exactions of a teacher and falls by the wayside on the way to a degree. As Bismarck contemptuously remarked, such a one may join the profession of the untrained—journalism; political journalism continues to be an avenue to power in modern societies.

There are famous cases in which a severe deprivation relatively late in life has led to furious concentration upon power. Joseph II of Austria, "the revolutionary emperor," as Saul K. Padover has called him, was transformed into the grim figure of his later days not only by the untimely death of his beloved wife but also by the shattering humiliation of the discovery that his wife had not loved him. (8) A turning point in the hitherto somewhat unfocused career of John Bright was the critical experience of losing his first wife. Three days after her death Richard Cobden after offering words of condolence said: "There are thousands of homes in England at this moment where the wives, mothers and children are dying of hunger. Now, when the first paroxysm of your grief is spent, I would advise you to come with me, and we will never rest until the Corn Laws are repealed." And he did.

The same principle of using power for compensatory

purposes is exemplified in the undeniably important role of real or fancied physical limitations. (9) We remember the "withered arm" of William II of Germany, attributed to a fall when he slipped out of the hands of an English governess. And there was the short stature of Napoleon. We think, too, of the rapacious ambition of the palace eunuchs in the history of both China and the Near East. The fact or the fear of sexual inadequacy has been a bitter spur to the accentuation of power. Queen Elizabeth was plagued by persisting doubts as to her attractiveness and capacity as a woman. The smallpox that scarred Mirabeau turned him into an object of distaste to his father. The ugliness of the famous political orators, Lord Brougham and John Randolph of Roanoke, was undoubtedly a factor in their political intensity. The infantile paralysis that Franklin D. Roosevelt overcame left him a better disciplined and more power-centered personality than when it struck him down. Like many men who escape death, he achieved the inner self-confidence and perspective of one who lives "on borrowed time."

An early illness or enforced period of inactivity has sometimes played a more important role in the development of personality than even the determination to overcome handicaps. Delicate children have gained knowledge from reading that aided in the consolidation of political aims. Mazzini, for instance, and William Pitt, Jr., appear to have made productive use of early invalidism.

The intensive study of infancy and childhood, conducted by modern methods of careful record taking, has underlined the decisive importance of the early years in shaping the structure of personality. These data have prodigiously documented and refined ancient maxims about the crucial significance of the early years. The data go in the direction toward which we have been pointing. The accentuation of power is to be understood as a compensatory reaction against low estimates of the self (especially when coexisting with high self-estimates); and the reaction occurs when opportunities exist both for the displacement of ungratified cravings from the primary circle to public targets and for the rationalization of these displacements in the public interest; and, finally, when skills are acquired appropriate to the effective operation of the power-balancing process. (10)

The factors that accentuate power in the person likewise operate in molding the response of the group. In general, according to our theory of power, we expect that power will be accented by groups when they expect it to protect them against deprivation or to restore and expand their influence. At the same time adverse estimates of the self must not be overwhelming, or the resort to power will be blocked by sentiments of utter hopelessness, such as have demoralized certain folk cultures after exposure to the deprivations inflicted by the carriers of modern industrial civilization. Expectations favorable to the use of power in the future are strengthened by the recollection of successful applications of power in the past under similar circumstances. The paradigm case is Prussia in particular and Germany in general. To Prussians it was power in the disciplined form of military violence and, to a lesser extent, diplomacy that brought the group from the sandy barrens of the North Prussian plain to the startling eminence of a middle-sized and then a great power. Was Germany crushed by the Entente in 1918? Prussia had revived after being crushed to the earth by Napoleon and the French; and in the more distant past by the trauma of the Thirty Years' War and the depopulation and partition of the German people. The self of the representative German incorporated the symbol "German" and with it the entire myth of German history, character and destiny. The extremes of self-admiration and self-debasement present in this mythology provided a potent determiner for the accentuation of power in the name of the collective self throughout the group, and for the service of the central myth by the power-seeking personality. (11)

In reviewing the theory of political personality outlined in this chapter it may be useful to match it with the *homo politicus* of much popular and scientific tradition. (12) The image I refer to is that of the power-hungry man, the person wholly absorbed in getting and holding power, utterly ruthless in his insatiable lust to impose his will upon all men everywhere. Suppose that we refine this traditional conception into a speculative model of the political man comparable with the economic man of the older economic science.

The following postulates can be laid down (the numbering is arbitrary):

1. He demands power and seeks other values only as a basis for power.
2. He is insatiable in his demand for power.
3. He demands power for himself only, conceived as an ego separate from others.
4. His expectations are focused upon the past history and future possibilities affecting power.
5. He is sufficiently capable to acquire and supply the skills appropriate to his demands.

It is evident that the model, thus constructed, can only be completely satisfied by a world ruler, since the fifth postulate includes the idea of success. Since there have been no world rulers, this model can be used to investigate no known cases. (However, there have been universal states, if we take the expression to mean that the "known world" was under the domination of a single power of overwhelming strength.) Therefore, we can profitably begin to revise the postulates for the purpose of fitting the model to illuminate a broader range of concrete circumstances.

We can, for example, withdraw the success postulate, which makes the political man omnipotent, and simply make him omniscient, in the sense that he always foresees correctly the power consequences of the moves open to him in any given situation. This makes it possible for the political man to remain less than a world ruler, if he is counterbalanced by other power operators who similarly exploit to the full their power potential on the basis of correct calculation. But to postulate omniscience excludes the very features of reality that most require investigation if we are to build up a body of knowledge related to human behavior. One of the most rewarding questions to raise about decision making is this: on what expectations are wars declared, treaties signed, diplomatic intercourse resumed, international organizations launched or other measures used? Unless we can understand the interaction of expectations upon demand (and identification) we are not far along in comprehending anything worth knowing about the decision process. The examination of such perspectives calls for knowledge about how they interact not only in the person but also in the group; and how a given set of expectations or demands or identifications is affected by other perspectives and by other factors in the sociopolitical process.

The third postulate prescribes a wholly egocentric personality, since all demands are made solely for the expected enhancement of the primary ego. Hence the *homo politicus* is not permitted to have a self (by which is meant a symbol structure included with the primary ego and given equal treatment). According to our speculative model, the perfect power type is wholly absorbed with advancing the value position of the "sacred me" (not "us"). Hence he sacrifices anyone and everyone at convenience for his power, and does not conceive of power as a means of advancing the value position of family, neighborhood, nation or any other group. If we allow unconscious as well as conscious demands to be included in our model, the psychiatrist at least is likely to say that this *homo politicus* is never found in nature, and is most closely approximated by a few paranoid psychotics or psychopaths. It must be admitted, however, that these are met in history in positions of power, as in the notable instance of "mad King Ludwig" of Bavaria who liked a bit of human blood in his hunting bag. (13)

Let us conclude by saying that while everyone is compelled to agree that this model of the political man of tradition does, in fact, perform a certain scientific purpose by highlighting some historical and contemporary figures, such as the "mad Caesars," the model is unsuitable for the most comprehensive inquiries into the decision-making process. The conception is far out of line with many known cultures, social structures and even crisis facts. The emendations and elaborations called for in relation to such circumstances are almost literally "too numerous to mention."

There is the danger, often exemplified in economic analysis, of choosing a speculative model, which applies to a few extreme instances, and becoming absorbed with the refined restatement of the postulates, rather than with exploring the varied phenomena of society. As one economist wrote when criticizing a book on economic theory by a colleague, (14) "On pp. 76–77 his marionettes start as 'normal human beings . . . familiar in a modern Western nation . . . acting with ordinary human motives . . . knowing what they want and seeking it intelligently.' But by p. 268 they have become 'mechanical automata.' " "Institutional economists" have attempted to absorb themselves in the context of concrete cultures and specific circumstances. But they have been rather slow in spinning a web of useful theory between the classical models of the perfect market and the many-colored tapestries of everyday life. In more recent times there are signs of a deliberate quest for speculative models of sufficient richness to further the interests of science and policy. (15)

Warned by this example, we use a theory of the political type that can be directly implemented with data of observation stemming from any concrete situation. Our political man:

1. accentuates power
2. demands power (and other values) for the self (the primary ego plus incorporated symbols of other egos)
3. accentuates expectations concerning power
4. acquires at least a minimum proficiency in the skills of power

The man who accentuates power is doing so *relative* to others, and therefore power personalities can be detected, by comparing them with standard expectancies for a culture, a social layer, a crisis or some other specified frame of reference. Besides accentuating power, it is recognized that the political type is not fully described until we know whether he is accentuating power in relation to one part of the self or all. We know that some identifications with the nation, for instance, guide and indeed swallow up the energies of the person. So far as the acquiring and exercise of skills is concerned, we provide only for some minimum degree of mastery which permits some measure of survival in the arena of power.

Our central picture of the political man, therefore, reduces the wolf man, the *homo lupus,* to a special pigeonhole. He is but one of the entire process by which primary motives are displaced onto public targets and rationalized in the name of public good.

IV. VARIETIES OF CHARACTER
AND PERSONALITY

WITHIN the broad stream of personal development that culminates in the political type, many variations occur. An inner tie is evolved not only with power in general but with particular manifestations of political life. Agitators and administrators, for example, may be distinguished from one another. (1) When the emphasis is upon arousing and sustaining widespread emotional response, the role is agitational, and the agitator seeks to acquire the appropriate oratorical and literary skills. If the role is specialized toward carrying on activities within an officially prescribed frame, the task is administration, which may be sought and prepared for, producing an administrative type.

Political specialization may emphasize certain perspectives toward change. Obviously demands for innovation can be basic or restricted in scope, and radical or moderate in method. The basic changes are revolutionary, and restricted changes are reforms. The most extreme positions in the spectrum advocate or pursue revolution by radical methods. Revolution can be directed toward introducing a new order or toward restoring a past system (counterrevolution).

It is a matter of common knowledge that political demands are affected by the hopes and fears that people entertain about what the future has in store for them. Will effort be rewarded? Will things turn out well even without effort, thanks to the nature of history or Divine Plan? Such expectations about the factual structure of the universe as it affects the value position of the self may exert a fundamental influence upon programs to support or resist change.

In many ways the most uncompromising denial that change can improve man's lot is de Maistre's: "It does not belong to man to change institutions for the better. . . . Hence the automatic aversion of all good men for innovations. The word reform, in itself and before any investigation, will always be suspect to wisdom, and the experience of the ages justifies this instinct." (2) Saint-Simon would have been justified in citing this as an example of his "stationary" type of opinion (the other two being "retrograde" and "liberal"). (3)

A. Lawrence Lowell made a more comprehensive typology of political perspectives by combining two kinds of expectations (estimates of the self in the present and in the future). (4) First, he separated people into the contented with their current lot and the discontented. Next, he separated those who are sanguine about the future (including human efforts at improvement) and those who are not sanguine. On this basis he came out with the following simple and workable scheme:

	Contented	
Sanguine	Liberals	Conservatives
	Radicals	Reactionaries
	Discontented	

(right side label: Not Sanguine)

Fruitful lines of inquiry are opened if we take this system of classification as a series of hypotheses. Lowell's formulation is that expectations affect demands, but he says nothing about demands influencing expectations. There is certainly substantial ground for asserting that those who *want* often adjust their statements of fact to fit the want. Very likely we deal with interaction rather than a one-way determinative relationship between expectations and demands.

It is not within the scope of our present undertaking to pass in review all of the political typologies that have been presented for serious consideration. Our aim is to link the study of political types somewhat more closely with the work that is being done on basic forms of personality development by scientists from several fields of medicine, psychiatry, psychology and social psychology.

CHARACTER TYPES

Temperament types, however, after the manner of Kretschmer (5) or Sheldon, (6) are not as close to our present concern as what are often called character types. (7) A character type is formed when a particular dynamism or set of dynamisms is relied upon to cope with the anxieties that occur during conflicts of development. How do basic character patterns operate in power situations; or, more generally, how is the accentuation of the power possibilities of a situation affected by the type of character? The temperament undoubtedly has a selective effect on character; but the correspondence appears to be far from perfect.

Varieties of political development are affected by two character types which are to be discussed at some length. (Brief observations will be made about other types later.)

Of special utility in accounting for specializations of

political type is the *compulsive* character, which is distinguished by the degree to which it relies upon rigid, obsessive ways of handling human relations. (8) Another type is what we call the *dramatizing* character. This term is not in general use but refers to several well-understood phenomena whose unifying feature is the demand for immediate affective response in others. The dramatizing character may resort to traces of exhibitionism, flirtatiousness, provocativeness, indignation; but in any case all devices are pivoted around the task of "getting a rise out of" the other person.

From what we have learned of compulsiveness, we expect it to exercise a significant effect upon the public targets and justifications which are substituted for the figures in the primary circle of the developing political personality. The compulsive character will select less varied objects for displacement and rationalization than the dramatizer. The compulsive inclines toward carefully defined limits and the well-worked-out ordering of parts; the dramatizer excels in scope and abundance of loosely classified detail. The hallmark of the former is the imposition of uniformity, while the latter tolerates diversity and excels in nuance. The compulsive desubjectivizes a situation, while the dramatizer remains sensitized to psychological dimensions; the one denies novelty, while the other welcomes it; one squeezes and compresses the dimensions of the human situation which the other complies with and allows to spread. The compulsive monotonizes the presentation of the self to the other, while the latter multiplies the faces and façades which can be presented to other persons.

What is involved can be made most apparent by reviewing three histories. The information herein summarized was obtained in the usual way by several procedures of investigation, ranging from psychiatric (or partially psychiatric) interviews, to the testimony of colleagues and intimates, and participant observation in ordinary life situations. (The customary precautions are taken to protect the memory of the subjects. Minor details have been altered, but the basic profile has not been retouched.) The three men ended their careers playing comparable political roles, since all became judges. But there are notable variations in political type. One is unmistakably an agitator, while another is basically an administrator. The third is a less specialized political leader. The administrator owes the peculiarities of his development in part to the compulsive character which he acquired comparatively early, while the agitator was undoubtedly a dramatizing character. The third judge had a less distinctive character type, although he was more closely related to the dramatizer than to the compulsive.

These men will exemplify one of the subtle dynamic processes by which established institutions are subject to change. There is a continual interplay between office and personality. At any given moment a complicated pattern of expectation and demand may be attached to an "office." To some extent perspectives may be spelled out in the authoritative language of a statute book. In some degree the office is defined by the perspectives of those who have the most direct working relationship to it, as superiors, opposite numbers or subordinates. Besides, there are expectations and demands made by those who have more remote or occasional contact, such as reporters, editors, group leaders, group publics or the general public. Hence the act of entering an "office" is to appear at the focus of attention of those who are predisposed to expect and demand rather definite modes of conduct from the office holder. In addition to demands and expectations, the office may be a focal point of loyal identifications on the part of many persons and groups.

The office holder acts selectively on the basis of the predispositions with which he enters in the new situation. If he is an agitational type, he tends to respond to agitational opportunities. If, on the contrary, he is an administrative type, he goes in the other direction. In either case the office changes, and the perspectives entertained about it are modified. Both Roosevelts developed the agitational possibilities of the presidential office, while Herbert Hoover underlined its administrative potentialities. A given trend may be reversed, as when William Howard Taft de-emphasized the impetus given to presidential leadership by Theodore Roosevelt, and Woodrow Wilson, in his turn, rejected the comparative inactivity of his predecessor and resumed the march toward expanding the office. (9)

Our interest in the following case fragments is, therefore, many-sided. Space constrains us to be overschematic and overbrief in alluding to many political figures. I hope that these fragments will provide a reminder of the fullness with which personality probes need to be made, since these extracts are the most extended case reports that it will be feasible to introduce in this book. Sufficient detail is offered to give an inkling of what is involved in looking into the developmental links between character type, political type and political role.

The procedure in presenting each history is to outline the consensus about the judge's official conduct among brethren of the bench and bar. Then follows a sketch of what an observer saw who watched the judge's behavior in the courtroom situation. After this comes some indication of the roles played off the bench in public or private political life. The next step is to examine the intimate life of the subject, including private evaluations and ambitions. Finally, the sequence of development is indicated, providing some clue as to how the person was seen by others and by himself. In general, the aim is to occupy observational standpoints of varying degrees of intensity (intensiveness-extensiveness) throughout the entire career line. (10) One standpoint is that of the *stranger* who describes the public image of the subject; a second standpoint is that of the *acquaintance-friend;* a third is that of the *intimate friend;* and a fourth is that of the *intimate scientist* (whether psychologist or psychiatrist). Without following the sequence too pedantically, the aim is to allow the political role to dissolve into the political type, and then into the character type.

JUDGE X

Judge X had an impeccable reputation for integrity. He was also regarded as exceedingly severe with offenders, and given to imposing higher fines and longer prison terms than his colleagues. In general, he was reputed to be a "government judge," meaning that he was strongly disposed to uphold the government in tax cases, as well as in cases involving narcotics, white slavery, kidnaping and the like. The exception was antitrust cases. The judge appeared very reluctant to "unscramble" big businesses or to hold businessmen criminally responsible for violations. On labor matters the judge was popularly tagged as "antiunion" on the basis of a small number of well-publicized situations in which injunctions were issued. Where civil liberties were plainly at stake, Judge X followed the "liberal" line more often than not. In a word, the judge was believed by the bar to be upright, severe in ordinary crim-

inal matters, friendly to big business and quite respect-
ful of the Bill of Rights. On the basis of detailed
knowledge of Judge X's life on and off the bench, I
believe his general reputation was well founded. For
instance, his integrity was often tested in connection
with bankruptcy cases, where the appointment of a re-
ceiver is an important factor and where existing man-
agements often try to perpetuate themselves by court
appointment.

In the judgment of the bar the written opinions of
Judge X were competent, though overcondensed as a
rule and colorless. Occasionally the opinion would labor a point exhaustively and (in the general view)
pointlessly. This was characteristic of what often went
on in the courtroom when a case was being argued.
Although a man of high intelligence, Judge X would
often get exceedingly concerned about some point that
failed to impress anybody else as especially germane.
A stickler for niceties, he would permit the proceed-
ings to get bogged down in the game of piling technicality on technicality. Attorneys complained privately that
the judge wore them out with his overinsistent and
rather nagging style.

The courtroom picture presented by Judge X was
one of great austerity. A little short, rather thin and sal-
low, the prevailing mood ran from sternness to controlled irritation. A strict disciplinarian, exceedingly
sensitive to noise or disorder, the judge was given to
admonishing spectators and counsel at the drop of a
pin. His forehead was characteristically knit into a
frown, and one of his brows twitched with such a reg-
ularity that it was doubtless a tic. The lips were tightly

closed, and the lip line was straight. Mounting irritation was expressed by frowning and by slight motions of the jaw that bespoke the grinding of the teeth. The voice was rather high pitched, and the s consonants were often spoken with great sibilance, and the explosive possibilities of the t and the p were not overlooked. Many observers got the impression that the judge was chronically alert, tense and full of suppressed annoyance. And this impression was strengthened by his occasional outbursts of irritable moralizing, and by the vitriol sometimes packed in his speeches when passing sentence.

Despite the hushed, sober and tense atmosphere of the courtroom, Judge X was not notably efficient in getting through the calendar. On the contrary, he was usually in arrears. It was obvious to those who worked with him closely that the judge worked hard on his opinions and read widely and well. But there was a great sense of strain continually present, an all-pervading sense of being driven and overworked. Humor and wit were almost entirely absent from courtroom or chambers.

The reputation of the judge went beyond the bar to the general public, chiefly because of the role played early in life during a reform administration when the newly appointed judge presided over sensational cases in which public officials were successfully prosecuted for bribery and other abuses of office. The judge was a clear if somewhat dull and pompous speaker, greatly in demand on civic and professional occasions. From time to time he lent the weight of his name to worthy nonpartisan campaigns, and was recurrently mentioned for elevation to the highest court in the land, or for a senatorship from his state. Behind the scenes his voice was listened to in party as well as in civic and professional circles.

Although he never disclosed his ambition directly, Judge X hoped to maneuver himself into a situation where he would be an "inevitable" and preferably bipartisan choice for a major elective office. (The truth about his ambitions came out in intimate interviews to be referred to later.) From an early time the judge fantasied himself turned to unanimously by his fellow countrymen as the man of the hour, the leader of unimpeachable integrity who would bring honesty, efficiency and justice into public life. In this purpose he was not entirely successful, but he was several times on the verge of an uncontested nomination. Often the judge would draw up elaborate instructions to himself, imagining that he was governor, senator or president. These were full of imposing ethical and legal slogans. Needless to say, these documents were destroyed without being shared with anyone else.

The home life of the judge was exceedingly formal, and although the more intimate facts were concealed even from friends, the emotional atmosphere was full of tension. For it was at home that the judge allowed himself much freedom in expressing his hostilities and in domineering over others. His wife was a colorless, though socially suitable, person. The judge regarded her as an incapable person and interfered in every detail of the household and in the rearing of the children. Opposed to disorder and a convinced apostle of discipline, he constantly criticized her alleged carelessness and overindulgence of the children. The youngsters grew up to be "disappointing," often failing at school and getting into disciplinary difficulties that were covered up out of respect for the judge.

From an early age the judge worried about his health and devoted himself to elaborate rituals in the interest of warding off the many bodily illnesses of which he stood in terror. His medicine cabinet was a well-equipped drugstore, and he experimented clandestinely with nearly every health fad from chewing his food until all meals were dragged out to unconscionable lengths to stuffing and scratching his interior with "roughage" to aid elimination. Beset by minor gastro-intestinal troubles, he finally sought medical assistance for a rather serious gall-bladder condition, in the course of which he was willing to talk freely about himself, partly from a growing sense of dissatisfaction with himself and his life. This was accentuated at the time by the physical and mental decline of his long-suffering wife and by the obvious shiftlessness of his children.

The development of X's personality is clarified somewhat when we learn that he was born into a wealthy and highly respected family in which the father was stern, melancholy and aloof, while the mother was religious, prudish, overtense and overprotective. At the mother's instigation—and this was established from direct testimony—the nurse tried to force the pace of cleanliness training, and imposed a severe regimen on the infant and child. Owing to the father's sensitivity, every effort was made to reduce noise around the home. As a lad Judge X had been subject to frequent illnesses (stomach upsets and headaches in particular).

In the course of a brief series of interviews Judge X recognized fully for the first time how much of his own career was related to his younger brother, whose arrival

had aroused his jealousy and whom he sought to excel
and to discredit in the eyes of mother and father. From
an early time X was excellent in his studies and devoted
himself to impressing adults with his brilliance and
trustworthiness. He became a rather withdrawn, hostile, cold and somewhat embittered youth with little
spontaneity and with a great sense of being goaded by
forces outside himself that kept him on the move. As
a child his rare outbursts of rage had been punished
physically; but he was especially sensitive when shamed
by his parents or subjected to withdrawals of affection
and privileges. As X learned self-control, he disciplined
himself in order to retain and enlarge his privileges,
frequently by putting his brother in the wrong.

An excellent though not a popular student, X went
through first-class educational institutions, and partly
through family influence soon became a partner in a
highly influential law firm. It was at this point that
crises of conscience began to interfere with his work to
a point that made it troublesome to complete any as-
signment. He resented the advocate's job of preparing
a brief for one side only and declared with much indignation that it was against his principles to twist and
turn in the preparation of a case for the sole purpose
of "blinding the eyes of justice" for the benefits of one
side. The senior members of the firm were disturbed by
this and finally hit upon a way out. They used political
influence to obtain a judicial nomination for this young
and overscrupulous partner. At the moment there was
a local reform wave in which civic associations were
passionately rising against the "scourge of lawlessness
and corruption" with which their city had been cursed.
With his well-known name and impeccable connec-

tions, X was an ideal candidate, won easily, and consolidated his public reputation as presiding judge in the prosecutions that soon began.

Looking at X from the standpoint of our basic conception of political personality, it is rather clear that his displacements from the intimate circle (and the accompanying rationalizations) were highly overcompensatory. Exposed to an early environment with notably indulgent and deprivational features, X was constantly struggling against aggressive tendencies provoked by frustration. Since it was impossible to express these tendencies directly without being overpowered and deprived of indulgences, aggressiveness was internalized in the form of compulsive strictness, busy-ness, rigidity (and light somatic conversions). But in some degree these drives were externalized in the form of burning ambition to excel by destroying the unworthy. Human relations became unspontaneous and calculated. Energy went into the making of plans for success in public life and for acquiring and applying the techniques that appeared to be the most instrumental. Relying upon compulsive mechanisms to hold his own aggressions in check, Judge X was attracted to the well-systematized authority of the bench, where he was given to excessive concern with legal technicality at the expense of the rapid administration of justice. Appealing solely to the conscience of the community, and having little warmth of personality, X's public career, distinguished though it was, fell short of his ambition. With the exception of his auspicious start in public life, he never came to grips with a crisis situation in which the conscience values (the mores) were uppermost, where he might well have been the rallying symbol. Actually, his range of ready identification with people was narrow, and neither imagination, training nor experience supplied him with much knowledge of the total impact of the decision-making process upon the life of society. He was unmistakably conservative in outlook, reflecting the standards of judgment prevailing in the upper-class circles in which he moved. (The protection of civil liberty, by the way, was a feature of this tradition.) His excellent talents were spent on drawing distinctions that made little impression on legal doctrine or on the public.

Clearly, the compulsive features of X's adjustment led him to select certain opportunities offered on the bench and to neglect others. He showed the capacity of the compulsive character to become preoccupied with detail and to allow the whole context to elude him. The atmosphere of the courtroom stressed the stern and fussy aspects of the judicial office. It was plain that the judge used the opportunities of his position to dehumanize the people who came in contact with him, especially on official business; and that beneath his propriety lurked a destructive contempt for himself and for others which betrayed itself in a chronic state of irritable tension. A compulsive character made an administrator in fact who daydreamed of becoming a versatile and commanding public leader, a dream that never came off, partly from the lack of effective capacity to project human warmth into casual and official relations.

JUDGE Y

In several particulars Judge Y presents a contrast to the colleague we have been considering. He was appointed to the bench late in his political career. People at large thought of him as a successful boss, and there were many protests against his elevation. But the opinion of the public and the bar turned more and more in his favor, and at the time of his death there was no judge with a higher reputation for integrity and fairness. Perhaps the clearest contrast with Judge X was in the imposition of sentences. Where X was ruthless, Y was benevolent. However, Y was not "soft," and he was not thought of as unduly sympathetic with the parties who were defending themselves against the government's prosecutor. On questions of taxation and business regulation, Y was far less "legalistic" than X and sought constantly for light on the actual economic and social consequences of the various practices upon which he was called to pass judgment. Partly because of his business experience (to say nothing of his political life) Judge Y was treated with special consideration by his colleagues of the bench and bar and was frequently credited with having "cut through the arguments" to the core issues. In litigation involving labor and management, he took a "middle way" and was looked upon by both sides as open minded. At first the bar had imagined that Y had long since "forgotten his law." But they were soon disabused of this notion and agreed that his opinions were cogently if not gracefully put together.

The atmosphere of Y's courtroom was in striking contrast with that of Judge X. Judge Y was ruddy, round-faced, bald and big. His voice was casual though distinct and musical. He made a minimum number of movements and displayed no tenseness. The impression was one of quiet mastery.

Courtroom habitués felt that the judge was particularly careful to reassure timid young lawyers or halting witnesses, especially if they were poor and Catholic. But they did not insinuate that the judge was antagonistic to the rich or the Protestants or the Jews. Many times he would take the direct interrogation of witnesses out of the hands of a lawyer who seemed to be asking clumsy questions or in any way confusing the witness. He was especially thoughtful of the foreign born, or of anyone who spoke with a foreign or an unacademic accent.

Actually the political career of Judge Y is a success story of no inconsiderable magnitude. He came up the hard, tough, rough way. He was reared in the working-class district of a big city and had been the leader of his neighborhood gang. The gang was predatory but not notably vicious or cruel. That is, the gang stole food and loose articles and fought with rival gangs, but became entangled in no systematic looting and had little trouble with the police or the community at large. Judge Y became a proficient boxer at the athletic club run by one of the political parties, and he and his gang were frequently used in election fights. Occasionally there was intimidation of voters or ballot-box stealing, but all this was taken as part of the game.

An older politician took a liking to Y, advised him to study law, and got him a soft job on the police force until he passed the bar. Then Y was "cut in" on a number of businesses that depended on political patronage, such as insurance, trucking and street-paving. By using advance information about utility extensions, he was able to invest successfully in real-estate developments. But he scrupulously kept out of "smelly" operations. For instance, he did not use squads of window smashers to demonstrate to the store owner that insurance was needed. He did not use his political influence to pass complicated building codes which could be used for extorting protection money from property owners. He did not take bribes, either to intercede with "political" judges or other administrative officials or to put through special legislation. Also, he did not profit directly from gambling, prostitution or dope peddling, although he often closed his eyes to what members of his political machine did.

It was not until well along in middle life, long after he had been a powerful boss, that Y began to dream of stepping from unofficial power to responsible public leadership. The change came largely at the instigation of his wife who had become socially ambitious and felt the stigma of being "Mrs. Boss." Under her prodding, Y began quietly to use his money to increase the prestige of his name. He used the usual channels, either directly or through his wife, contributing to hospitals which were the pet charities of the local dowagers (presently getting elected to various boards), contributing to the expansion of the medical school of an eminent local university, contributing to the symphony orchestra and the theater. In addition, there were well-placed donations to the activities of his church and fraternal orders. After these preparations, he put himself on the ballot and got elected judge. Judge Y had always been a fluent speaker, although not a major orator, and his public appearances were dignified.

Looking further back into Y's career, we find that he was subject to loving but earnest prodding by his mother. His parents were evidently happy and affectionate. The father was a skilled mechanic who was easygoing and outgoing and the mother, with a somewhat better education, determined that her sons should "amount to something" in the world and was continually strict and watchful.

It appears that Y incorporated much of his mother's ambitious, energetic, optimistic and friendly outlook and approached the world outside the family with confidence. He assumed family responsibilities when young, marrying a neighbor girl who was a great favorite of the community. She had much the same balance of ambitiousness and warmth that characterized his mother.

The accentuation of politics in the personality development of Y was less on the basis of overcompensation against low estimates of the self than in the case of many other leaders of whom we have knowledge. His environment provided indulgences for him as he went up the ladder, and it is quite possible that Y could have been thrown out of his job as boss or judge without "taking it too much to heart." He was, of course, exceedingly quick in recognizing where power lay, and although it was not possible to apply any measuring instrument, the trained observer could not fail to be impressed by the high level of intelligence he displayed in dealing with political problems. Part of the impression of ambitionlessness created by Y came from the great speed with which he foresaw political contingencies and prepared for them. Hence he usually maneuvered himself into a winning position before making a final move. (Deeper psychological analysis of Y was precluded by the fact that the only time available for talking intimately about his past was when he was laid up with an accident.)

The personality of Y was quite free of compulsiveness. Obviously he belongs to the dramatizing group we mentioned above, in the sense of responding sensitively to other human beings and of cultivating skills adapted to sustaining an emotionally significant contact. We find, for instance, that his range of emotional responsiveness in dealing with people easily passed through the entire gamut. He was reserved and friendly, deferential, humorous, witty, angry, reproachful, sympathetic, earnest. Y's affects flowed spontaneously in ways that knit people to him from all walks of life.

Judge Y's conduct on the bench was in keeping with the selective processes anticipated from such a developmental type. This was reflected not only in his benevolence, in the tendency to assist and take responsibility for the young or the handicapped, but in the alert and self-possessed way in which he explored the possible consequences of his decisions. He was not rigidly bound to cloud his eyes with technical arguments before he had a clear picture of the factual situation to which they were supposed to apply. Manifestly, the judge found it unnecessary to retire behind a pedestal or a technicality to protect himself from human or physical facts.

JUDGE Z

A more striking example of the dramatizing type may indicate some of the dangerous possibilities inherent in such a development. It was generally agreed that Judge Z had a keen intellect and was quite capable of following the most involved argument. As one man put it: "He's not like Judge Blank; Blank is lost after the first verb. Judge Z is usually ahead of you." At the same time the consensus among the older members of the bar was that Z was erratic in his judgment, often appearing to be wholly uninterested in the legal aspects of the case.

A common remark about Z was that he would "do anything for a laugh," or that he was a "publicity hound." He was invariably genial, though reserved, with the press, and the impression that he played to the gallery came from a few cases in which he did something popular and sensational. In each instance he had dug up some ancient statute and applied it literally— and with astonishing results. In these cases the ideas had been brought to his notice by a bright law secretary, or had been thought up by himself. He took great delight in showing up the "imbecilities of the law," as he called them in private. At the same time, in so far as he personified the majesty of the law, he was obviously impressed by the mantle and permitted no liberties to be taken with his authority. Significant, however, is the contradiction between this attitude and the occasional breaches of decorum in the courtroom and the private expressions of contempt for the law. The truth is that the judge would give an ear to any argument if it seemed to point toward startling consequences.

However, there is no evidence that Z thought consistently of the law as part of the social process, seeking to extend and maintain the values of the community. Although his opinions have been studied with care, few straight lines emerge. Actually the opinions present a highly varied patchwork. They were written in a rather florid style, studded with "color" adverbs and adjectives. The legal points were not systematically, but discursively, handled. As remarked before, his sole contribution to legal doctrine appears to have come as an incident of some startling application of a sleeping statute.

Taken in conjunction with the parties involved, however, the role of Judge Z in the administration of the law is somewhat clarified. In criminal cases he was "soft" with young offenders, "tough" with men in middle life, and exceedingly "soft" with the old. This comes out in the relative severity of the sentences imposed, and is confirmed by his conduct toward the parties in the courtroom (especially his tendency to dismiss cases).

Further inquiry into Judge Z's conduct in criminal cases reveals additional traits. His sympathies were, by all accounts, genuinely enlisted by calm, suffering victims; but he was equally impressed by self-possessed defendants. He was exceptionally "antigovernment" whenever the prosecution failed to "personalize" the victim, especially when the latter was young, physically attractive, or notably self-possessed, even defiant. He was promptly repelled—and visibly overreacted—at any sign of hysteria among women; and he was touched by unaggressive old people, especially if they were poor and suffering.

In civil cases Judge Z showed no well-thought-out attitude toward industrial concentration or government control of business. There were evidences of bias against bigness—against the giant corporation—but he had no confidence in regulation or socialization. However, toward the end of his career, there was an unmistakable drift toward favoring both strong and expanded government. Trips abroad impressed him with what nationalistic and totalitarian regimes were capable of accomplishing. Also, as the years went by and Russia seemed to consolidate, he began to admire collectivization and to speculate about what was later called "the wave of the future." In private talk he began to say that the corruption of American politics and business was so complete that only a rebirth, a reawakening led by young men, could save the country.

Judge Z was not noticeably tall, but he conveyed an impression of being above average height on account of the thinness of his skull and the creases that lined his face. His hair was parted differently than was common in his part of the country and slicked down. The most conspicuous feature of the countenance were luminous eyes, which he used with dramatic effect when he fixed counsel, witness or juror with his gaze. There was a frequent play of expression around the corners of his eyes, and the lids were often lowered or raised to convey what could be variously construed as interest, boredom, disbelief, certainty, doubt, amusement or repugnance. The lashes were long and the brows jutted over rather receding sockets. One mannerism was the raising and lowering of the eyebrows. His mouth was not firmly closed and the lower lip was full and red. Occasionally he would purse or lick his lips, and sometimes pass a hand over his mouth and chin in a light, caressing movement. Usually he was overdeliberate. He seemed to initiate any expressive act as though it were worthy of being carried through with dignity. This was especially noticeable in the use of his long, tapering fingers. Many of his wrist gestures were graceful; he often allowed his hands to hang limp from the wrist. A musical, flowing voice added to the total expressiveness. But there were jerky interruptions in voice and gesture which signified to a trained observer that some impulses not in harmony with the deliberateness were not far below the surface.

So far as clothes were concerned, Judge Z was conspicuous. He wore colors usually associated with actors and other less drab professions than the law. Often the hue of his shirts was arresting; and the lapel flower might be, too. The cut of his suits and the style of his shoes, to say nothing of his snappy hats, were even foppish. There was a faint aroma of hair tonic—he was freshly barbered daily—and of perfume.

To a close observer of Judge Z's behavior in the courtroom it was apparent that he was given to playing favorites among counsel, parties and witnesses; and that he used his supple features and hands to convey his attitudes to the jury. His favors would sometimes pass suddenly from one counsel to the other; and he would flit from calm to flashes of vexation. Witnesses, too, were subjected to mercurial treatment—sometimes being reassured by the sympathetic voice, sometimes rasped by intonations of distrust. There were many examples of sudden reversals of favor toward a counsel who had received especially deferential treatment through several trials. Most of these instances involved young lawyers. The judge, in dealing with elderly men, was very indulgent, particularly if they were down at the heel and were neither aggressive nor querulous. Often he selected Masters in Chancery from this group of broken-down lawyers, commenting to his secretary that law was a risky profession and even the humble, if honest, deserved a break. But the counsel who tried to browbeat the Court, or the distinguished practitioners who adopted a strong and condescending tone, these he blocked at every turn. He usually maintained great decorum in the courtroom, but permitted himself irony, sarcasm and contemptuous wisecracks when confronted by the behavior of the type mentioned. At such times he would grow pallid and press his lips in a straight line, digging the nails of his fingers into the palms of his hands.

Clues to the personality of Judge Z can be gleaned by examining the role he played off the bench on public occasions. He was a favorite orator at party gatherings and patriotic celebrations. On the platform he was decidedly theatrical in style, fond of deliberate movements and dramatic pauses, such as the ancient trick of reaching for a glass of water. His mellifluous voice was pleading, commanding, exhorting, expounding, chiding—it was capable of expressing every nuance of emotion. The vocabulary was flowery, full of emotive language about morality, justice, love of home and country. He broke into poetry without effort and told stories with enormous gusto and mimetic skill. His perorations at Fourth of July celebrations were famous, and he was very effective at pathos. He could denounce or defy. But he was actually more effective as a glorifier than as a prosecutor.

Often in his speeches Judge Z referred to his contacts with great names, and he did go abroad enough to be received by the heads of foreign states and to be decorated. (There were large blocs of voters of European origin in his constituency.)

Although the judge evaded any direct avowal even to his intimates of specific political ambition, it was obvious that he was a popular leader who might step from the bench to the Senate at any time. He was absorbed by the problem of political power and read the lives of famous men, analyzing the technique that enabled them to "shape history." As he grew older the ordinary ladder of politics in this country failed to arouse his imagination. Stimulated by developments abroad he speculated privately on the possibility of organizing a young men's movement in the United States, with himself at the head, beginning first as a secret order. He welcomed speaking engagements around the country that would bring him in contact with young people, and kept on the lookout for promising lieutenants. In particular he considered the possibility of launching the secret society with the support of industrialists in mining and in the capital-goods industries, who he believed were particularly afraid of bolshevism. Many owners and executives were, he believed, in the reserve corps of the army, and he hoped to gain the informal support of the military for his movement. He kept physically fit, and even in later middle life was always sun-tanned and athletic, especially in an individualistic sport like tennis. He sun-bathed a great deal and paid strict attention to weight and diet.

In his own home the judge did a great deal of formal entertaining. His wife was older by a decade, but he kept a certain fondness for the motherly, if somewhat limited, woman. He found her, as he once phrased it to intimates, as restful as an old-fashioned hammock. At the same time her slow mind, limited outlook and slightly depressive temperament bored him. All during his married years he maintained a very discreet though active sexual life outside the home. The women were usually beautiful, exuberant and sophisticated. He enjoyed the thrill of pursuing a new woman, especially if he knew that another man was after her. He was inclined to grow indifferent as quickly as a woman grew "demanding," as he put it. He gave lavish gifts and was alienated by any sign of deep or lasting affection ("possessiveness"). Because of his own charm, this occasionally led to difficult situations, from which he was able to extricate himself by ingenuity and ruthlessness. His more abiding attachments were with youths to whom he turned, as he sentimentally put it, feeling like an old Greek hero.

The information about Z thus far summarized enables us to form a working model of a dramatizing personality. First of all, his intense craving for deference is evident. In court he managed to keep in the center of attention by the use of many subtle devices, such as permitting many shades of expression to cross his countenance, playing off one counsel against another, and abruptly shifting his favors. His dress and demeanor were bids to look and like; and this demand went far beyond the courtroom or his home. He keenly craved deference in the form of power, respect and affection; he perfected many skills and sought opportunities to get what he wanted.

To the trained eye Z's public appearance showed a great many exhibitionistic and homosexual trends. Although quite aware of his sexual interests, Z was not aware of the degree to which they influenced his judgment in a great many situations which he did not think of as specifically sexual.

For instance, he displayed many signs of overreaction against submissive tendencies, notably in the form of sudden hates, especially of assertive personalities, particularly when he began by feeling amiably disposed.

Furthermore, it is apparent that he made use of his polished manner to keep people at a distance and to reduce the emotional stresses of friendship among equals. His intimacies were with women and youths, not age mates.

Physical virility was an exceptionally strong interest throughout Z's life, including athleticism and sexuality. There is ample evidence of soaring ambition, especially revealed in the partial planning of a national movement to seize power. When drunk—as he occasionally was among intimates—he regularly bragged of his virility, of his superiority to other men, and of his ultimate destiny of ruling America and the world.

In this connection it is worth taking note of his double attitude toward playing an authoritative role. On the one hand was the ambition to play the judge to perfection and to rise to yet more authoritative positions; on the other hand was his hostility toward authority, revealed by his occasional tendency to make the court ridiculous with outbursts of levity, by his joy in ridiculing statutes and precedents, and by his persisting unawareness of his own social values. Although married, he refused, in the beginning, to have children, despite the hopes of his wife, and by the time he reluctantly agreed, his wife was too old. In short, he did not assume all the responsibilities conventionally attached to the marriage institution. Also, he was dependent upon his wife's money, and spent freely. Occasionally he would fantasy about resigning from the bench and "cleaning up" in private practice. He had no doubt he could do this, because most of the lawyers who appeared before him struck him as "dopes." Judge Z was able to indulge his cravings to be supported and admired (with comparatively little effort on his part) when the indulgence was coming from a devoted woman or from someone to whom he felt superior on grounds of age, sex or intellect.

His driving ambition and extreme deference cravings, can be interpreted as means of overcoming certain deep doubts about the self, doubts about being fully masculine.

The earlier history of Z throws further light on the genesis of his pattern of personality. His mother was a schoolteacher who had rather "come down in the world," as she believed, by marrying a laborer. Actually her husband was a highly skilled mechanic, but he was not the banker, doctor or lawyer whom the community thought she would marry. This middle-class woman, then, flouted the conventions. But she had no intention of being the wife of a "dirty-fingered mechanic." Partly with the help of her savings, and most certainly as a result of her pressure, Z's father left his trade and became a salesman, thus joining the white-collar, if not the professional, class. Actually the husband seems to have been an easygoing person who did not greatly resent having a strong executive in the house. He did, however, show signs of strain occasionally by getting drunk and abusive, or by staying away longer than necessary on trips and, as neighborhood gossip put it, "running around with other women." The mother, meanwhile, was intent upon the future career of her only son and pushed him hard to do well in school, which he obligingly did. He was praised and encouraged continually for any bright thing he said or did and from an early time acquired many ways of making himself acceptable to older people. He could recite, sing and be generally charming from the earliest years. He became very skillful in playing his parents off against each other, so that they were rivals for his affection. During early school years he became conscious of some contemptuous attitudes in the community toward his father, but these were modified by respect for his great physical prowess and by appreciation of his joviality and gifts. At the same time the father's absences sometimes gave him the sense of being rejected and unloved; and the occasional outbursts of drunken rage both terrorized him and confirmed his doubts about being loved. Although strict, the mother was free with praise, and looked after Z's physical needs and tastes with constant pride. She appears to have been prudish and to have supervised the boy's play contacts very closely. Apparently Z had little opportunity to gang up with other children for fear he would acquire what were vaguely called "bad habits."

From these data it appears that Z was given every opportunity to be loved and admired, even though this was made conditional upon striking achievement. At the same time the boy acquired some doubts about himself and definitely ambivalent attitudes toward authority. It is significant that he never fought back when cuffed by his father but inhibited any expression of rage, feeling merely shocked and helpless even when his father attacked his mother. The mother, too, was careful to insist that he must under no circumstances "flare up" against his father "who didn't really mean it." Z learned to rely on such techniques as patience, followed by sulking withdrawal of affection, succeeded by a gradual giving in to being wooed with renewed expressions of love—and new gifts. In adolescence came a series of circumstances which gave him a precocious start on his political career. As a boy orator he was much in demand and made the acquaintance of a powerful political boss who took him up as a protégé (including sexual intimacy). In the boss there was a powerful hero of the sort Z longed to depend upon, and from him came an unceasing stream of indulgences, which eventually included elevation to the bench.

The history of Z clearly shows the ways in which the agitator bends the opportunities open to him in official and unofficial positions according to the special dynamism of his personality. The bench is to some extent a stage; and it was Z, not Y or X, who magnified the potentialities of the bench for publicity. In any official position, there is an opportunity to play the role of a strong and benevolent authority, or to interpret authority as despotic, erratic, pedantic, inefficient and querulous. It was Y who incorporated within his own personality the conception of himself as a strong, yet benign, authority, who most fully realized these possibilities during his years on the bench. Judge X, on the other hand, thanks to his compulsiveness, emphasized certain despotic, pedantic, inefficient and querulous possibilities. It was Judge Z who most directly and flagrantly tended to cast the whole institution into contempt by his search for notoriety and by a form of erratic conduct different from that of X.

AGITATORS (11)

The agitational type (developmentally stemming, for the most part, from the dramatizing character) is obviously well adapted to crises of revolution and war in a society where automatic obedience cannot be taken for granted. Modern personality study provides us with means of arriving at a better understanding of the long line of agitational figures who have captured the loyalties of the oppressed and dishonored through the ages. However they diverge in degree, such agitational figures possess an exceptional sensitivity to the emotional orientation of others. One of Hitler's greatest assets, for instance, was his awareness of positive and negative attitudes among his collaborators. I remember long ago interviewing an early collaborator of Hitler's who provided a clue to this dimension of the fuehrer's personality.

"For several years I was fascinated by the fuehrer," said my informant, "and believed that the liberation of Germany from the incubus of dishonor and capitalism depended on Hitler. I was in continual contact with him in conferences, and I was usually among the small number of those who were asked to remain and talk some more. One day, to my surprise, Hitler did not ask me to remain; and I suddenly realized that for several weeks past there had been a growing sense of discomfort on my part with the Movement. I had never put it into words to myself, much less to anybody else. Hitler had sensed that there was something about me in relation to him that had changed before I knew it myself."

Hitler, like Judge Z, had early learned to gauge the slightest emotional undercurrent of those around him, doubtless as a means of playing off his mother against his father in the tense emotional atmosphere of his home.

BUREAUCRATS (12)

Compulsive characters are less versatile in adapting themselves to changing receptivities around them, since the compulsive mode of dealing with human beings is to disregard them by developing a set of rigid molds into which they are assumed to fit. When these dynamisms are dominant, as in the case of Judge X, the characteristics become exaggerated in the direction of the petty bureaucrat, who is trussed like a fowl in red tape. A more fundamental characteristic of the "bureaucrat" (than red tape) is his avoidance of responsibility. At first glance the bureaucrat appears to be a compliant tool of authority and to magnify himself by becoming one with authorized power. But this is to overlook the most significant dimension of the personality. The man who says he won't "stick his neck out" is not fully capable of playing an authoritative role. On the contrary, his level of hostility is such that the seeming devotion to the established way of doing things is counteracted by unrecognized forces within him. The self is not capable of playing a fully authoritative role connected with government because the unconscious demands on the personality are to destroy authority. These demands counteract the ostensible, conscious intention of the individual to be an upright judge, an honest public servant or a conscientious official. One manifestation of hostility is the constant weeding of a crop of doubts and queries about how rules are to be understood. All this appears at first glance entirely plausible. Nobody doubts that rules are ambiguous because they must, after all, rely on words, and words are notoriously inept tools for the task of communication. But doubts and scruples multiply. There is not only delay and uncertainty; there is "passing the buck up higher." All this easily defeats the survival interests of administration and undermines the authority which is presumably being most punctiliously served. In fact, government is knifed by the undisclosed hostilities of frustration; and, for the highly compulsive personality, all human contact, indeed all living, is well adapted to sustain a considerable degree of frustration. (Restrictive in this sense are the limitations of clothes, of demeanor, of hours, of tasks. Even the elementary functions of the body contribute to the inharmonious mixture of half-liquidated impulses that sustain tension.)

Hostility toward authority is rather clearly expressed in the "bureaucratic" tensions that rise in the process of interpreting authority. Not only is there the appeal to higher or more numerous instances: there is intense jealousy of the outcome, jealousy that one's own preferences may be set aside for those of another (brother), or, more attenuated yet, that one's preferences may be thought to have been disregarded by someone when the judgment is ultimately made.

A disturbing fact about compulsiveness is that it takes color under plausible arguments. Hence the intellectual life; and especially the dialectical professions of philosophy, law and theology, for instance, are shot through with strands of compulsiveness that impede the effective use of the mind. One consequence is the attrition from within of a doctrinal system by the complication and eventual undermining of the basic postulates. Presumably out of zeal to complete the logical symmetry of the system, new contradictions are brought to light. Not infrequently the refutations are less convincing than the objections that have been brought out, and that are presumably being disposed of.

DETACHED CHARACTERS

The foregoing remarks have been about the significance of compulsive and dramatizing characters for the varieties of political personality found in society. Other character types are of no little dynamic importance and may be referred to with at least a few passing comments.

Resembling compulsiveness in some surface aspects is detachment, which can be taken to refer to the dynamisms by which all affects that are admitted to the full focus of waking awareness are tamped down and deprived of intensity. We are, of course, talking of a basic dynamism and not a mature attitude like objectivity. Also it is not a question of extreme clinical conditions in which there is a turning away of all interest from the world, followed by absorption in fantasy, accompanied by great indifference to what is happening. The detached character, it appears, has undergone a structural change in the way he is related to his own loves and rages, with the result that the full dimensions of these affects are screened from consciousness. Such persons are not necessarily torpid. On the contrary they may manifest high intellectual skill and great curiosity, as if all the intensities that are gone from other spheres found expression in the pursuit of enlightenment. The extreme instances can be "killers without affect," or a kind of epileptic remoteness from full participation in the affective possibilities of a human relation. No doubt the color perceptions are unlively; and the life of the mind proceeds, so to speak, in a room with gray walls and taupe rugs. In the detached character type, when intelligence is high, it is possible to fake affectionate warmth, but the curtain can fall at a moment's notice. Because of seeming warmth and affectivity the detached type can even be mistaken for the dramatizing character. What this signifies is simply that intelligent persons can recognize signs of affective expectation in others and play up, much as the deaf man learns to read lips and to mingle smoothly with those who are not hard of hearing. The evolution of the detached character is at least partially known. Very likely the significant point is the simultaneous level of love and rage and fear that has been experienced in certain critical situations, and which has left something that might be described as an enduring "stasis" (detachment). (This is consonant with the general theory of how certain crucial constellations of affect can lead to a continuing undertone or tide of depression, elation, compulsiveness.)

From detached characters useful judges, arbitrators, conciliators, diplomatic negotiators and scientists can be recruited. At the same time, the absence of lively emotional states can lead to calm, pitiless, destructive conduct. I surmise that when we know more of the inner lives of political figures who have been able to survive as advisers or ministers during times of great insecurity and change, we shall find many genuinely detached types. (Fouché? Some of the famous diplomats?) The highly intellectual "fanatic" who is often classified with highly compulsive fellow fanatics may, on examination, be revealed as a detached character. (Calvin?) (13)

V. POLITICAL REALITY AND
THE UNCONSCIOUS

By THE intensive examination of personality in politics we become aware of the frequency with which unrecognized factors present in the personality of the politician handicap his success. Power holders may deliberately relinquish their position and retire; but we now speak of those who want power. Overwhelming circumstances may liquidate power; but external influences are not germane to the present point. Men and women have often had brilliant careers for a time in politics, yet they have brought blight upon themselves and upon those who believed in them because of the warping effect on judgment and action of certain unconscious tendencies. Without intending to give up power, they have imperiled or lost it. The enormous variety among political figures is strikingly exemplified when we compare them in terms of the realism of their decisions. The result is to cast into high relief one group of persons who consciously seek power in spite of unconscious tendencies that handicap them.

IMPAIRED WORKING ABILITY

Impaired working ability is often one of the indications that incompatible tendencies are at war within a personality. Emperor Charles V was unable to control his gluttony, despite injurious consequences to his health. Alcoholism has often been described as an occupational disease of the practical politician. (King Wenzel of Poland appears to have been one of the few rulers who lost the throne very largely through alcoholic excess. However, the number of powerful persons who have undermined their position by addiction to drink is legion.) Every time we obtain deeper insight into the complex dynamics of alcoholism, we learn more about a great many politicians. It has become almost a commonplace to discover that persons with excessive demands for deference (and some continuing low estimate of the intimate self) turn repeatedly to this particular drug. And we have seen that if our basic conception of the power-accentuating personality is correct, politicians come from this very group. There are grounds for believing that persons recruited from the dramatizing character type turn readily to an oral indulgence like drinking. (But so ubiquitous is the excessive use of alcohol that it is fruitful to look into the special function of alcohol in the different character formations in various culture settings, social strata and crisis periods.) (1)

Neurotic incapacity to concentrate or arrive at conclusions has imperiled the careers of able and successful men. General Bluecher, co-conqueror of Napoleon, is a textbook instance of this sort of thing, frequently succumbing to morose and torpid spells in which thought and action were equally out of the question. The evidence in his case, as in that of most historical figures, is too fragmentary to allow of thorough interpretation. (2) But in many less distinguished and more accessible persons, neurotic limitations are known to be directly related to the incompatibility between the power role which the person plays and some unconscious drives within the personality. Although inclined toward power, the person is also afraid of it. *Unrecognized fear of playing the authority role* is a dynamic predisposition of the greatest importance. (Further factors are essential to explain why a *neurotic* symptom rather than some other form of expression is evolved in order to resolve anxiety.) The analysis of personality development reveals such an astonishing range of opportunity to be afraid of power that the puzzling question is how so many people are able to get away with it. After all, it is in the name of authoritative persons and forces that curbs are put and enforced on the growing child. Not only does this imply a continual stream of deprivation emanating from authority, but secondary complications arise when such losses are first met by responses (like anger) which in turn must be relinquished. Even the parallel stream of indulgence which is supplied by, and in the name of, authority does not in this mixed setting invariably support friendly images of authority. For the attributions made by the one who receives a gratification may be to some other or incompletely authoritative image.

We know enough to justify the hypothesis that where there is hostility toward playing the authoritative role there is a clash in the images of authority which have been incorporated into the self. We saw, especially in the case of Judge Z, evidence of latent antagonism to the playing of an official role. Provisionally we assigned some of this to the incorporation into the self of images of being a victimizer and also a victim (stemming from the parental constellation in the primary circle). In Z, however, the subsequent anxieties were acted out rather than met by neurotic internalization.

NEGLECT OF POWER FOR OTHER VALUES

Neglect of power for other values is a reason for political failure in cases that are literally too numerous to mention. It is commonplace that the pursuit of affection can lead to the neglect of power. But sexuality and sociability are by no means the only rivals of power. Michael VII, the eleventh-century Byzantine emperor who used the scholar Psellus as an adviser, devoted himself to learning and allowed military defenses to deteriorate to a point that encouraged insurrection and foreign invasion. We are concerned with the point that neglect of power may spring from tendencies that are unrecognized by the person in question and that include hostility or fear of power. The dynamic source may be the same internal hostility that, in the cases mentioned above, found an outlet in neurotically impaired working ability.

ALIENATION OF SUPPORT

Neglect shades over rather quickly into the positive alienation of support by conduct that is overtly provocative of others. Nero, for instance, fancied himself an artist and horrified conservative Roman sentiment by performing in public. Iknaton became so absorbed in establishing a new religion that he seems to have lost all touch with the realities of power, even when the unity and integrity of Egypt were threatened. The idea of launching a new religion appears to have been originated as a tactic of statecraft by his immediate predecessors, who saw that the royal power was imperiled by the priests of the then current religion. But Iknaton set these plans awry by "taking religion too seriously." (3) He may well be among the great and good men of human history; but there is no doubt that he was out of touch with power realities, yet was compelled by his inner needs not to give up but to close his eyes to the crumbling away of power. Examples of this sort give practical point to cynical-sounding maxims: "Among politicians the esteem of religion is profitable; the principles of it are troublesome." (4)

> A ginooine statesman should be on his guard,
> Ef he must hev beliefs, not to b'lieve 'em tu hard. (5)

One of the important insights of modern personality analysis for politics has been the discovery that provocative behavior is often one of the means by which the environment can be goaded into inflicting deprivations upon a self that has unrecognized demands for self-punishment. In these instances it is not a question of conscious conflict between the necessities of power and standards of right and wrong (rectitude). (When the conscious problem is posed in such terms, the unconscious dimensions may have another significance.) Hence we are not referring to writers and politicians who have been acutely aware of the incompatibility of "reasons of state" and the claims of morality. (6) When we speak of unconscious guilt feelings, of course, the reference is to facts that may give incredulous surprise to the one who has them. I suppose all of us have had experience with some "tough guy" who, when given psychiatric aid in some jam, learns with amazement that he is driven by an "excess of morality." (7)

The low estimate of the self against which the demand for power is an overcompensating (and partly unsuccessful) reaction may not concern guilt so much as shame. Arrogance is often traced to an image of the self as contemptible, ridiculous, dishonorable. The adverse evaluation is in terms of respect more than rectitude. The dishonorable self is, in effect, self-sentenced to destruction by an inner court of honor, and the individual is compelled to execute himself indirectly by challenging a more potent knight who is sure to accomplish his defeat and death. In the light of what we now know we can better understand the self-destructiveness of Pausanias, the brilliant Spartan leader who won the battle of Plataea against the Persians and who commanded an allied fleet that reduced Cyprus and Byzantium. His domineering attitude alienated the allies and aroused the apprehension of civil authorities in Sparta, so that he was eventually put to death.

In addition to arrogance, power holders often undermine themselves by provoking revenge against the terror and degradation which they impose upon others. In some instances the recorded excesses are so marked that it is evident we are dealing with a psychotic. Shah Mahmud went so far as to order the massacre of the entire nobility of Persia, together with all surviving princes, and large numbers of the soldiers and inhabitants of Ispahan (1724–25). In the fourteenth century Mohammed Tughluk, who gained his throne in western India by parricide, became infamous for ferocity and indiscriminate cruelty. He was given to the wholesale extermination of revenue collectors, perhaps a worthy object in itself; but he appears to have set exorbitant quotas. We are not astonished to hear that this "half-mad military genius" finally provoked rebellion.

But terror is not to be dismissed lightly as an instrument of power, with the snap judgment that it shows an excessively sadistic motivation. It is always difficult to pass a balanced judgment on the rationality of killing, torture and humiliation. No friend of human dignity is biased in favor of these weapons. But no friend of truth will deny that men of quick intelligence often see that they must use violence and impose disgrace as economic means to the ends of power.

Consider the case of Mohammed Ali and the method by which he got rid of one of the greatest obstacles in his way to becoming the effective ruler of Egypt. In 1811 he invited the Mamluks (an armed force accustomed to making and unmaking viceroys) to a banquet in the citadel of Cairo. All were killed save a few who managed to escape. Not until 1847, however, did Mohammed Ali become so deranged that a regency was set up.

In many cases we believe that there must be a relatively strong tendency to enjoy the imposition of suffering on others, or power would be given up, since the cost in affection or rectitude is excessive. Think of Abbass the Great of Persia who had one son murdered and two others blinded. Irene, the empress of the Eastern Roman Empire about the time of Charlemagne, had her son taken and blinded when an army revolt put her in control. Cleopatra murdered her younger brother (Ptolemy XIII). Stephen Dushan, the Serb ruler and hero of the Middle Ages, began his career by strangling his father. Karageorge, the Serb leader and dynasty founder who lived at the end of the eighteenth and early nineteenth centuries, personally dispatched no fewer than 125 men who angered him. It is believed that he killed his father when the old man refused to flee with him to Hungary at a dark period in his fortunes.

All these examples are apart from the killings that are called wars (and not murders), revolution, suppression of rebellion and crime, and law enforcement. Nothing is said about mutilation, imprisonment, compulsory labor, starvation, or the casualties that can be attributed to the use of violence as a weapon. (8) The reminder of the facts of violence and the expectation of violence gives pause to anyone who likes to imagine that the use of physical ruthlessness is always a sign of sadistic motivation rather than of a rational mind.

CHOICE OF INADEQUATE PERSONNEL

In some ways unrealistic factors in personality manifest themselves most clearly in the choice of inadequate personnel. Strong men too often have weak successors, whether in government, business, churches, universities, professional associations or—perhaps above all—in family life. The scientific study of personality has laid bare many of the dynamisms by which too many parents deform their children, too many politicians maim their protégés, too many business leaders surround themselves with yes-men, too many university professors pick third-rate minds, too many churchmen choose windbags, and too many professional associations select stuffed shirts. At the same time we often see the near-miracle of brilliance following hard on the heels of mediocrity, decency succeeding decay, boldness following pusillanimity and wisdom foolishness. Our scientific task is to acquire more knowledge of the factors whose moving equilibrium brings about these results.

IMPACT ANALYSIS

That unconscious components of the personality result in poor personnel selection is dramatically obvious in some cases, as when unrecognized emotional factors lead to the selection of protégés who betray their sponsors. It is possible to obtain insight into the rationality of the personnel selections of a decision maker without knowing him personally. The procedure is to examine the personnel with which men surround themselves. You find the image of the person in the company he picks and the contacts he makes. We might call the reconstruction of personality by the study of persons chosen and sought the *technique of impact analysis*. It is the technique of studying "the men around Hitler" or "the kitchen cabinet."

Leaders often operate in situations where the personnel is imposed upon them. As one harried war administrator put it to me, "My chief problem is to get results that I don't care much about, from people I don't care much about, with facilities I don't much care for." Actually, however, there are enough selections and contacts to register more or less distinctive and accessible profiles. Consider the following sample situation.

The choices made by this administrator were almost at once intelligible in terms of a clearly understood task and a clear record of preparation for the job. But if you looked carefully several revealing points began to emerge. His trusted secretary was tense, meticulous, orderly, neat, prompt, prim, slow, worried and given to tearful upsets under great pressure. Sociable and expansive persons of the same age level as the administrator or older were gradually edged out, leaving young people who were conscientious technicians but devoid of significant contacts outside the office. They came from the same small-town background and the same modest educational institutions from which the boss had come. Employees with higher social status or graduates of the better-known colleges did not remain long; nor did convivial souls who liked the cocktail, bridge or poker circuit. Some of those who were on closest terms with the boss and his wife (a former grammar-school teacher in a small town) went regularly to church and Sunday school. The administrator mixed with other permanent officials and paid comparatively little attention to cultivating any other group. An analysis of his contacts outside the office showed frequent social relations with individuals much like himself in the Budget, Civil Service, and old-line agencies.

This administrator was a protégé during the war of a prominent public figure who had a varied collection of close associates wherever he was, in or out of government. Some were bright young lawyers brimming over with smart ideas. Many of the lawyers were from the same upper social class background as the big boss and had a great network of connections in Washington and elsewhere. The big boss was unmistakably an agitational personality, continually in the public eye until he went back into private life. To his surprise and chagrin he was succeeded by the rather cautious, compulsive person whom I have described. When promoted, the new man carried with him his covey of equally cautious, compulsive types, and the entire enterprise ceased to be a significant source of initiative.

This is a sequence often met. A dynamic, agitational, dramatizing figure puts into a key administrative spot a useful and specialized tool, and "forgets" to notice that he is grooming a successor who is too limited and rigid to preserve an enterprise that depends on new ideas and successful promotion. An analysis of the top man's contacts showed that he spent little time with his administrator, being almost wholly absorbed with "idea men" and with top officials, Congress, the press, group leaders and especially personal friends holding a wide variety of key spots in and out of government. He was wholly without awareness of the fact that he was condescending toward "drudges" of low social origins and modest cultural skill. Hence he did not pay sufficient attention to facts that would have enabled him to think and act realistically about a part of the total problem with which he was vitally concerned, namely the perpetuation of an activity into which he had poured colossal energy. (9)

Although it is no great exaggeration to say that we have learned more about human beings in the last fifty years than in the previous history of mankind, this does not mean that we know as much as we need, or even that we have fully applied the methods whereby we can know more. We certainly must not claim too much. We continually come across situations that pique our curiosity and challenge our best ingenuity in devising educational and personnel methods. For example, Basil the First of ninth-century Constantinople stands out as a remarkable instance of a leader who, despite his origins, conducted himself with that integration of power with other values which is usually called "statesmanship." Yet in his formative years Basil was without formal instruction and was exposed to the most demoralizing environment. He climbed to the throne by unscrupulous bloodshed.

Consider the education of Charles James Fox. He was treated by his father, Lord Holland, with extreme indulgence. The lad was permitted to choose his school, and at the age of fourteen was taken by his father to the Continent where he was encouraged in dissipation and gambling. Many other successful leaders, on the other hand, have come up on the austerity plan.

Recall the phenomenal success of John I of Portugal, an illegitimate son of Peter I who established a dynasty in the fourteenth century by leading a revolt that successfully drove out the regent. John had five outstanding sons, of whom Henry the Navigator was one. How can this remarkable showing fail to impress anyone who is acquainted with the dreary record of misfits so frequently found in the families of every social level?

SITUATIONAL ANALYSIS

Throughout our treatment of political personality development, we have spoken of the career line of the individual. From a scientific point of view the career looks less like a line than a chain of zigzags or spirals in a continuing sequence of situations. This is also the way life is experienced "from within." Looking over one's shoulder, there are the abandoned plans and operations that might have altered the course that was taken. Looking ahead, several bends, corners and levels are always coming into view as new goals, alternatives and contingencies are thought of. And the scientist sees a career, not as a sequence of words and motions produced by an isolated manikin whose output per hour is clocked, but rather as an unceasing interaction in which the participants provide one another with an environment to which, and in which, they respond on the basis of the predispositions with which they entered the situation.

The *responses* are the events for which the scientific observer is seeking an explanation, like winning elections, obtaining appointments, successful advocacy of statutes, getting favorable administrative rulings, winning of verdicts in courts, or destroying the enemy's will to resist. These are the *decisions,* marking the outcome of a process of shaping power in the interactions that take place in the *arena.* In explaining any category of response, the scientific observer looks in part at *environments,* which are the events impinging upon a responder while he is in a situation. Thus decisions may be affected by the testimony, debates and deals that are made in the session of a legislative body. That part of the environment which gets to the focus of attention of the responders is the *milieu.* The parts which, though having an effect, do not get to the focus of attention are *surroundings.* (In relation to a legislative body as a whole, for instance, a speech is typically part of the milieu, while a secret deal, involving a few members only, is part of the surroundings.)

Predispositions are the ways that participants are oriented to respond when they enter a situation. It may be that legislators arrive definitely committed to a party program, or at least to follow the leaders of some party.

It is evident that the career line of any person can be divided for study into as few or as many segments as are appropriate to the problem in hand. For some purposes it makes sense to consider all life situations after birth as constituting one vast environment in which responses occur. If so, the "predisposition" refers to the organism at birth. Beginning with bodily types describable at birth, we might discover the "power expectancy" of such types. But it is obvious that this is not likely to give very useful results. Hence we can more profitably proceed by selecting situations of more limited scope. We might, for example, decide to study the responses (the decisions) of the justices of the Supreme Court during their entire time on the bench. It is possible to define "liberal" or "conservative" for the purpose of classifying these responses. Then we consider the environment to which the justices are exposed on the bench, including arguments in court and experiences off the bench. Next, we look into the predispositions with which the justices ascended the Supreme bench. (10)

It does not need to be demonstrated that this basic procedure can be applied to any desired cross section of life and carried to any degree of refinement. Each case before a justice might be given separate treatment, the *response* being the decision, the *environment* whatever impinges upon the justice while the matter is before him, and the *predispo-*

sition being the potential responses as established on the basis of data obtained for the period before the justice was exposed to the case.

Our conception of the political type and its many variations must be checked and perfected as it is applied to selected situations throughout the entire manifold of personality and culture. (11) It is obvious that we do not assume that the political type is born with a jet mechanism that propels him with unerring accuracy from the cradle, say, to the Kremlin. Situations need to be examined from culture to culture, social stratum to social stratum, crisis to intercrisis; and within these broad frames of reference. We can examine all institutions concerned in shaping and sharing power, wealth, respect (and any other value), and select representative situations for study. At each point we define the responses to be called power and undertake to discover whether those who accentuate power are persons predisposed to use skills which they justify in terms of a common good which is alleged to follow when demands are made on public targets of the same sort as the demands displaced from the primary circle. (Motivations-Displacement-Rationalization.)

The way is then open to probe into the variations of political personality that occur when a dramatizing, compulsive or some other character type pursues power. As these relations are progressively clarified, policies become possible that are designed to foster forms of political personality capable of realizing the goal values of democracy. In our society I join with those who advocate policies favorable to the dignity of man, which means the goal values of a democratic commonwealth. Our problem, therefore, now passes from the contemplative analysis of political personality to the frame of reference of active policy.

VI. DEMOCRATIC LEADERSHIP AND THE POLICY SCIENCES

WE COME, finally, to the specific needs of democracy. In a democratic commonwealth, power is not only shared but subordinated to respect for the dignity of human personality. In common with every form of political society, democracy depends upon rearing, choosing and supporting leaders who can protect and perfect its values and institutions. The principal expectation contained in democratic ideology is that it is possible to attain universal democracy by bringing into existence on a global scale the equilibrium that has repeatedly been achieved in more parochial communities. The democrat identifies himself with mankind as a whole and with all subordinate groups whose demands are in harmony with the larger loyalty. The technique appropriate to democracy comprises all the skills of thinking, observing and management that contribute to the survival of the commonwealth, and all the methods by which a social equilibrium in support of democracy can be achieved and maintained.

Unless leaders with the personality formation appropriate to democracy are supported by the community, it is obvious that the equilibrium essential to sustain the democratic commonwealth cannot be maintained. Hence, on analysis, the problem of democratic leadership to which we are addressing ourselves becomes nothing less than the task of dealing with society as a whole. To meet our definition of democracy, leaders must be drawn from the community at large, rather than from a few social strata. The term "elite" is used in descriptive political science to designate the social formation from which leaders are recruited. In nondemocracies the elite is limited. It is composed, perhaps, of a few landholding families, or the families of the main merchants, manufacturers and bankers. The elite may be restricted to the families of the chief party officials, or government officials, or officers in the armed services (including the political police). Democratic leadership is selected from a broad base and remains dependent upon the active support of the entire community. With few exceptions every adult is eligible to have as much of a hand in the decision-making process as he wants and for which he is successful in winning the assent of his fellow citizens. There is no monopoly of power in a ruling caste when such conditions prevail, and the whole community is a seedbed from which rulers and governors come. The elite of democracy ("the ruling class") is society-wide.

The distinction between leaders and the elite enables us to avoid the confusion that often arises when someone points out that government is always government by the few, whether carried on in the name of the *few* or the *one* or the *many*. James Bryce made the point in these words:

In all assemblies and groups and organized bodies of men, from a nation down to a committee of a club, direction and decisions rest in the hands of a small percentage, less and less in proportion to the larger size of the body, till in a great population it becomes an infinitesimally small proportion of the whole number. This is and always has been true of all forms of government, though in different degrees. (1)

The proposition is true when it is understood to mean that "government is always government by a few *leaders*." It is false if it is construed to mean that "government is always government by a highly restricted *elite*," and that democracy is by definition impossible. In a modern large-scale society the leaders do exert an enormous impact on war and peace and on major questions of domestic policy. But democracy is not extinguished unless a community-wide basis of selection and responsibility is done away with.

It should not be denied that the long-run aim of societies aspiring toward human freedom is to get rid of power and to bring into existence a free man's commonwealth in which coercion is neither threatened, applied nor desired. This is the thread of anarchist idealism that appears in all uncompromising applications of the key conception of human dignity. When Engels wrote of the eventual "withering away of the state" he was voicing the hope, though not necessarily the certainty, of the radical democrat. In our day, however, the probability that we can reduce power to the vanishing point seems very remote indeed. The urgent task is to chasten and subordinate power to the service of respect.

HUMAN DESTRUCTIVENESS

The problem of achieving and sustaining a dynamic equilibrium consistent and compatible with democracy can be examined in another perspective. It appears that what we have called the task of democratic leaders and the elite is equivalent to the whole problem of curbing human destructiveness. Our conception of democracy is that of a network of congenial and creative interpersonal relations. Whatever deviates from this pattern is both antidemocratic and destructive.

Evidently man's great enemy is man; or, speaking more precisely, human destructiveness. Human destructiveness is of two kinds: destructive impulses and destructive practices. Practices are destructive when they express or arouse destructive impulses. Destructive impulses are the initial phases of acts which, if brought to expression, destroy congenial and creative interpersonal relations.

A social equilibrium free of destructiveness would be rid of many of the traditional scourges of mankind. Men would not knowingly kill one another, whether in war, revolution, uprising, criminal violence or criminal repression. Men would not kill themselves. Human beings would not mutilate and chastise one another.

If these glaring specimens of destructiveness are brought to the vanishing point, a profound transformation will have occurred in the major cultures of the globe. It is impossible to abolish acute destructiveness without altering the equilibrium of the entire social process, since such acute disturbances mainly give vent to stress that has cumulated through the social system as a whole. If stress is to be curtailed, it is essential to scrutinize closely the links in the chain of social life which at first glance may not appear destructive. The banker who makes a commercial loan in the ordinary course of business, the board of directors that retains a monopolistic advantage for the company, the trade union that condones restrictions of production, the pressure group or trade association that sustains a trade barrier may unwittingly contribute to a wave of happenings that spell collective inflation and collapse. A social practice is destructive which provokes intense concentrations of destructive impulse, although most of the process occurs under circumstances in which the participants neither see nor seek these results.

HEALTH AND DISEASE

This examination of destructiveness in man and society must have a familiar ring to physicians. It applies to society as a whole the pattern of thought that has enabled medicine to distinguish between disease and health. Every classification of a process as "disease" calls for the applying of a standard pattern of integration which is "health." We can speak of human practices and impulses as pathological when we discover that they destroy or threaten to culminate in the destruction of creativeness and congeniality in interpersonal relations.

It begins to appear, therefore, that the leader-elite-destructiveness problem is closely equivalent to the problem of disease and health, seen in the perspective of mankind as a whole. It has become something of a commonplace that modern medical sciences have progressively enlarged the frame of reference that is considered to be relevant in classifying phenomena as either healthy or pathological. In many circumstances, of course, excellent results can be obtained by dealing with a very limited context, as in classifying and treating a simple abrasion of the skin. But when blood supply and thermal regulation are thought to affect the picture, either by slowing down or speeding up the recovery process, a much wider frame of reference is taken into account by the physician, a context large enough to include the body as a whole.

The frame of reference is often enlarged to take into consideration events that occur outside the body and that directly affect what goes on within it. The discovery that small organisms introduced from beyond the surface of the body can perform a necessary, though not a sufficient, role in the disease process opened up two modes of attack upon the prevention of disease. Either receptivities were altered within the body or conditions in the environment were changed.

For many purposes the medical sciences have paid special attention to the part of the environment composed of human beings. Certain destructive sequences inside the body have been traced to difficulties that arise in interpersonal relations. Certain somatic disorders are precipitated when partial responses initiated as part of the total response to the human environment grossly interfere with one another. Partial processes connected with mobilizing the body for flight may clash with partial processes connected with sexual mobilization or angry assault upon the environment. Conflicts of this kind may reach a level that disrupts healthy equilibrium and gives rise to demonstrable changes in the soma.

Modern medicine has a formidable list of the changes in the body that occur when difficulties in the social context of response bring about destructive interference among partial processes. As a reminder of the vast scope of these relationships, note the following organization of topics (by Leon J. Saul) (2) in a review of current knowledge:

Gastrointestinal disturbances: disturbances of appetite and eating; bulimia, Anorexia Nervosa; nervous vomiting; oesophageal neuroses

Disturbances of digestion: stomach neuroses; peptic ulcers

Disturbance of the eliminative function: chronic diarrhea, spastic colitis, mucous colitis, ulcerative colitis; chronic psychogenic constipation

Cardiovascular disturbances: essential hypertension; cardiovascular neuroses

Respiratory disturbances: asthma; hay fever; laryngitis, common cold

Skin disturbances

Endocrine disturbances

Epilepsy

Headache

Genitourinary disturbances: bed wetting; genital function

To this list we must add the following (from the topics covered by H. Flanders Dunbar [3]):

General metabolism and heat regulation

Special sense organs exclusive of the skin (eye, ear, other senses)

Bones, including odontology

Gynecology

The impact of the human environment on the soma goes under the name of psychosomatic medicine, and while this term has great merit, it has limitations. The term "psycho" does not carry with sufficient definiteness the connotation of social (interpersonal), despite the fact that the disease context is a response relationship among people. It is when something goes awry in the person-to-person context that the somatic disorders appear which are the subject matter of psychosomatic medicine. Somatic disturbances follow disturbances in the pattern of social contact. We might rechristen the branch of medicine that concerns itself with the bodily manifestations of a disease process arising in defective interpersonal relations and call it *sociosomatic* medicine.

The fact is, of course, that physicians have been unwilling to confine themselves strictly to the somatic results of a diseased interpersonal process. Often a sufferer turns for aid to the physician when there is no discoverable somatic source of distress. Or the complaint comes from members of the environment who regard the person's conduct as intolerable, yet somehow different from the behavior one would call criminal.

This is the type of concern that has led to the rapid broadening of the context taken into account by some branches of modern medicine, notably psychiatry. Complaints lacking a demonstrable somatic basis raise many puzzling conceptual issues about the scope of medical science and practice. How is it possible to speak of disease at all under these circumstances? Why not turn the patient over to the police as a behavior problem? If he has learned to function badly in society, is it the physician's job to straighten him out?

Often physicians have been able to relieve the sufferer without changing his somatic pattern, enabling the patient to find ways of responding in a fashion that is acceptable to the people constituting a given environment. But by itself the discovery of a few workable devices for returning sufferers to ordinary society is hardly a satisfactory state of affairs, since experience shows that the range of therapeutic intervention is enormously widened if there is theoretical understanding of the disease processes involved.

Hence psychiatrists, too, have come gradually to the view that the appropriate frame of reference for behavior difficulties is not the body but the context of interpersonal relations. But this viewpoint, in turn, raises several disturbing questions. Reference was just made to the patient who is returned to a community where he again makes acceptable responses. Does this mean that the physician takes the layman's conception of "acceptable response" as the standard of discrimination between disease and health? If so, which layman? Does one take a poll of the laymen of the Bronx or

Westchester or of the East Atlantic states? And why stop there? Should one refer the matter to the United Nations?

I think it is fair to say that the notion of applying the conception of disease and health to the entire social process fills many conscientious members of the medical profession with alarm. It appears to plunge the physician-scientist into partisan controversy and to reduce him to the level of a layman. Obviously no one can classify any given pattern of government, business, church or scientific activity as "diseased" without committing himself to a set of value preferences. Shall the physician-scientist simply call his social convictions "health" and dismiss his opponents as "sick"? If the physician is a Republican, are the Democrats ill? If the physician believes in capitalism, is he free to call socialists and communists sick? If he believes in God, is every atheist and agnostic pathological? If he believes in monogamy, are all other forms of marriage social pathology? If he believes in the United Nations, is everybody on the other side diseased?

Many psychiatrists, at least, have tried to resolve the difficulty by invoking the concept of functional disorder. Even where no somatic disturbance can be found, the failure of response is attributed to the interference of partial processes with one another, an interference involving that acutely dysphoric state known as anxiety. Thus not all functional difficulties of response are taken as within the province of psychiatry. If the response is "bad learning," for instance, such as the formation of a "criminal conscience" on the basis of early development in a "criminal environment," the person is, by definition, excluded from the offices of the psychiatrist and handed over to the courts and the police. But wherever it can be shown that anxiety complicates the response that clashes with the demands of a certain social environment, the person is eligible, on the definition, for treatment.

It is no news to any specialist that there is no consensus at the present time on the meaning of "anxiety." Some psychiatrists use the term not only to cover a so-called basic anxiety to which everyone is subject, but regard the task of coping with anxiety as fundamental to the development of every person. (4) When usage is this broad, there is no social practice existing in any culture which may not contribute to anxiety, and which the physician therefore may not be called upon to scrutinize from this point of view. That war, revolution and similar crises are formidable instigators of anxiety (thus broadly conceived) hardly needs to be demonstrated. Physicians who give the term anxiety the wide connotation just referred to are equipped with intellectual tools that enable them to approach the task of exploring the entire social process for the sake of discovering pathological sequences. From this perspective, whatever invokes anxiety is pathological, with or without somatic difficulties.

The anxiety criterion, however, is a rather indirect justification for treating the person who is free of somatic troubles but who nonetheless has some anxiety. The inference is that it is solely because anxiety can precipitate bodily difficulties that it is within the province of the physician.

Some physicians prefer a more direct approach to the prevention and cure of pathological social processes. War, for instance, is admitted to be a disease manifestation, not because it can be shown to contribute to anxiety, which in turn can bring about bodily ills, but because it is a relatively destructive folkway. After all, war kills people, destroying their somatic integrity, which is presumably the key criterion of traditional medicine in deciding what is healthy and what is diseased.

That organized medicine has been slow to prepare itself

for the study and abolition of war and revolution as methods of social change is not surprising. The kinds of fact-gathering and analysis pertinent to the problem are not within the conventional skills of the medical scientist and physician. That, of course, is no serious argument against changing the basic training of the profession, or against the development of new specializations. Drastic shifts in medical training and practice have occurred in the past, and may be expected to occur again.

The most striking position is taken by physicians who assert that medical inquiry has shown the dependence of the bodily and mental integrity of the person upon affection and respect. This approach has most in common with the problem of democratic leadership and eliteship (to say nothing of the reduction of human destructiveness). Scientists and physicians who adopt this view are therefore committed to explore the entire social process for the purpose of discerning and abolishing whatever impairs the self-respect of human beings.

This is a value-oriented medicine which is explicit about more values than somatic well-being. It includes the value of respect as a goal and a condition of healthy interpersonal relations. Among the medical disciplines the nearest neighbor of this branch is sociosomatic (psychosomatic) medicine. We are speaking of social psychiatry, which is set off from neuropsychiatry. (This is what I take to be the recommendations made by General C. B. Chisholm to his colleagues.) (5)

THE POLICY SCIENCES OF DEMOCRACY

The implication is that there is room for a social psychiatry of society which is in fact the social psychiatry of democracy. It becomes one of, if not coterminous with, the developing sciences of democracy, the sciences that are slowly being evolved in the interest of democratic policy.

Controversial? Yes. But this need not be held against it. Some of the most outstanding developments in medicine have been controversial. Let us dismiss those instances in which the scientist or physician had data of observation on the basis of which he attacked current dogma and folklore. Semmelweiss, for instance, was not arguing with his opponents over whether mothers and infants should be saved. The issue was not one of value orientation, but of observing and interpreting data. However, the medical psychologists (psychiatrists) who argued that certain patients were not possessed by demons, or being punished by an avenging God, were joining issue on value grounds. Even if it could be shown that some of these unfortunates could be restored to everyday life, *should* they be brought back? Was this not impious dabbling with Divine plan? (6)

Note that I have not yet discussed the tactical question whether clarity in these matters will help or hinder the attainment of results. Honest men have argued that to talk about social psychiatry and to recognize that it starts with value judgments (preferences) is to undermine the authority of the physician and to reduce him to the status of a layman who is matching biases with other laymen. They fear that this will destroy confidence in the medical profession. If we talk about democratic medicine, does that open the way to the denial of medical aid to antidemocrats? Must everybody carry a card in the proper political organizations, or an F.B.I. certificate, before he can get treated for ulcers or cut into for kidney stones? In a future war, if the enemy is believed to be antidemocratic, will our physicians let his wounded die?

These questions are not to be dismissed without a serious answer. Respect for the bodily integrity of everyone has undoubtedly had great humanizing results. It has helped to keep alive the bonds of human feeling in the bitterest clashes of war and revolution. No matter how many physicians failed to give adequate attention to American prisoners in the last war, or to Japanese prisoners, there were many who served them. I think no person of democratic sympathies will deny that minimum respect for human dignity enjoins the alleviation of unnecessary suffering and the maintaining of bodily integrity (well-being).

Surely these points are not too complex to make plain in public or private. Hence I doubt that there is important evidence that the aims of social psychiatry will be damaged by the open declaration of its intentions.

That social psychiatry overlaps what is customarily called the domain of the social and psychological sciences need occasion no concern. Who, in this heyday of semantic sophistication, need be disturbed when it is realized that special groups in our society use different names for the same reference, or even the same name for different references? (7) The problem is translation, which is a matter of equivalency, and this can be accomplished by explicitness of definition.

Social psychiatry, then, is one of the policy sciences, along with law, education and the social disciplines at large. *Sciences are policy sciences when they clarify the process of policy making in society, or supply data needed for the making of rational judgments on policy questions.* Hence the policy significance of each specialized branch of inquiry varies greatly from time to time and place to place.

If we get rid of the standoffishness that has kept men of knowledge apart in our civilization, we can more conveniently come together in research teams that are capable of contributing the knowledge needed by democratic policy. Every expert brings with him valuable instruments for the common task. The psychiatrist, to choose an obvious example, has ways of interviewing that elicit data which are usually buried out of sight of the economist who knows how to gather and examine price figures. The man trained in the laboratory and clinic may have little knowledge of the social institutions with which the historian, political scientist or sociologist, for instance, may be equipped.

The conception of the policy sciences has been enormously stimulated by the period of deep crisis in which mankind is living. After World War I the liberating symbol in American social science was method, "scientific method." Certain leading figures saw that the advance of knowledge about human relations was held back by the astonishing lack of communication among the many specialists who were engaged upon various sections of the vast terrain. (8) From this lack of contact came many unfortunate results in the form of wasteful duplication, neglect of problems lying between the accepted subdivisions of academic labor, and failure to disseminate the most useful procedures for gathering and processing data. During World War I itself, potential contributions from social scientists were neglected, partly from lack of confidence in their methods. At the same time, the war gave a great impetus to certain branches of social inquiry, which were the fields whose methods were most confidence-inspiring to physical scientists and engineers. Psychological testing, for instance, made great strides in serving the war, and economists were much in demand.

Out of the experience gained in the emergency came the initiative that culminated in the founding of the Social Science Research Council, with emphatic stress put upon the improvement of method and the cross-fertilization of all specialties touching upon human relations. By means of fellowships, grants-in-aid, conferences and advisory services the general aim was furthered.

The integrating and technicalizing movement among the psychological and social sciences had some measure of success. In World War II a larger selection of specialties was ready to be drawn upon than in War I. Attitude measurement, for instance, was relied upon to a previously unimagined extent.

Today we are living in a world of ever-deepening shadow, in which basic democratic values are challenged as never before and in which even the survival of the human species is at stake. Under these circumstances it makes sense to develop a strategy of using our limited intellectual resources for the defense and extension of our values. The term "policy" is used to indicate the need of clarifying the social ends to be served by a given allocation (including self-allocation) of scientific energy. (9)

By laying the accent on policy we are not attacking objectivity. On the contrary, objectivity is put where it belongs, which is in the service of goal values. Policy includes not only breathless, short-run objectives: policy also comprises intermediate and long-range aims and it is in relation to the latter that scientists can make their greatest contribution. There is a broad field in which the scientist can try out new theoretical models and test new procedures of factgetting and processing. It is thinkable that the students of human relations have achieved a degree of self-confidence and proficiency in which "method" and "objectivity" can largely be taken for granted, and hence that questions of intellectual-social strategy can receive needed emphasis. The policy perspective, it must be repeated, can be applied by the individual specialist to alternatives that confront him at any given moment. At the same time, this way of thinking can be used by the voluntary and official associations of science.

It may be objected that the selectivity involved in policy thinking has long been applied to the practical needs of government, business and other institutions, and that the aims sought have been antidemocratic in intent and scientifically trivial in result. But the use of policy thinking by antidemocrats for petty purposes does not exempt the democrats from using their best judgment in economizing scarce intellectual resources for the purpose of accomplishing the comprehensive goals of human dignity. On the contrary, one of the indictments of intellectual life under democratic conditions has been the failure to carry to a higher stage of perfection the sciences of democracy, the mobilization of knowledge which alone provides the intelligence on which rational democratic policy can be founded.

There is, of course, a general science of society which can be stated in terms that include democracies and despotisms. Such comprehensive formulations have been made, and they can be usefully revised in the future. The pressing need, however, is for the mobilizing of motive and skill for the purpose of elaborating the missing links in the chain of analysis and observation which bears most directly upon the maintenance of the social equilibrium of democracy.

It should not be supposed that the policy-science orientation is a totally novel idea among scholars. Something of the kind, for instance, was in the mind of John W. Burgess when he visited Europe at the request of President Butler to gather ideas about the future organization and personnel of the political and social sciences at Columbia. (10) The expression "Faculty of Political Science and Public Law" was intended to embrace a very large part of the then recognized academic branches of social science. And the conception was present not only of advancing the boundaries of knowledge for its own sake but also of performing a policy-clarifying and advisory function. Unfortunately the term "Political" had somewhat dubious connotations then as now, seeming to imply petty partisanship. Actually the term that would have carried the most fruitful long-range connotations is "Policy." Oddly enough, this is the closest English word to one of the German terms from which Burgess made his choice. He was, of course, right in avoiding a literal translation of the word meaning "the sciences of the state" (*Staatswissenschaften*), since the technical expression "state" has always suffered in the United States from the fact that the word is not in popular use to designate the nation as a whole. The word *Politik*, however, was available; and it might well, even preferably, have been translated as "Policy." If Columbia had organized a "Faculty of the Policy Sciences," the term would have stood more successfully for the underlying aim of the institution. And today (if I may make a gratuitous suggestion to the eminent controllers of the destiny of that great university) a change in name would celebrate, emphasize and inspire.

The policy sciences as we see them today cut across the traditional division of intellectual labor, and therefore do not entirely coincide with what John W. Burgess had in mind in his time. At the core is the theory of human behavior, the theory of society, which includes a systematic account of the factors controlling personality and culture. Contributions to this comprehensive theory come from every branch of knowledge that throws light on the interaction of living organisms in their environment. The decision-making process itself provides the principal frame of reference in relation to which the general theory of response is formulated. Comparative social history and sociology (anthropology) are involved here. Special attention must be given to the ways by which the institutions of power can be managed, whether by the use of words directed to large groups, by the use of promises in direct negotiation with individuals and group representatives, or by the use of goods and services, or by the instruments of violence. These are the four principal fields of policy, often referred to as propaganda, diplomacy, economics and strategy. (11)

Around the central body of theory and data about the process of decision comes an ever-shifting group of specialists who preoccupy themselves with the processing of all human knowledge for the use of a free society. The specialist may be an expert in somatic medicine; or psychiatry; or physics, biology or any subdivision of the enormous corps of men and women who work in the physical sciences and technology. Perhaps the background of the policy thinker is not academic, in the sense of an accredited command of science, philosophy or the humanities. He may be an experienced man of action who possesses the qualities of intellect that qualify him to reflect upon his life and to put his observations into words that illuminate our understanding of policy. The policy sciences welcome anyone whose skill and experience are joined with objectivity and communicativeness, and who can aid in making clear the bearing of it all upon democracy.

THE INTELLIGENCE FUNCTION AND RATIONALITY

What we are calling for is a more perfect intelligence function which embraces the highest as well as the humblest forms of pertinent knowledge on the basis of which rational decisions can be made. Decisions are rational when they do, in fact, enhance the probability that preferred future events will occur.

Today it is even clearer than it was a few years ago that the automatic triumph of democracy cannot be taken for granted but must be the outcome of a more brilliant and consecutive application of determination and intelligence than ever before. Democracy is subject to the fundamental laws of human behavior and in order to endure must sustain more optimistic expectations of value fulfillment than nondemocracies. (Human beings behave on the basis of expected net indulgences over deprivations, unconscious as well as conscious.) The issues of everyday politics are fought out in countries that are not wholly democratic, and such democratic features as are present are often made the scapegoat for unsatisfactory results that should, more rationally, be ascribed to the surviving nondemocratic characteristics of the community. In view of the many hurdles in the path of the statecraft of democracy, even the modest claim of Fisher Ames for a republic, which is often adapted to democracy, is open to grave doubt. "A republic is a raft that will never sink, but then your feet are always in the water." (12) This is too optimistic. You not only keep your feet wet but you *can* sink and drown. There is no magic key capable of winding up a democratic society so that it can spin indefinitely. In a far deeper sense than our forefathers had in mind democracy depends on "eternal vigilance."

Democracy is not safe even where there is a high degree of devotion to the doctrines of freedom and to the key symbols of shared power and shared respect. It is essential to maintain a *continuously high level of effective agreement about the policies that implement the goal*. Hence the policy-making processes of a free society, which necessarily imply debate and difference, can be disrupted by disagreements that continue while action is deferred, until mounting levels of unrest bring about revulsion against democracy.

CATHARSIS IS NOT ENOUGH

It is true that a democratic order can protect itself by catharsis, and that the system is particularly well adapted to the harmless discharge of affects. From the standpoint of the social order, acts perform a catharsis function when they dissipate hostile impulses with no disruption, or even significant alteration, in the social system as a whole.

We know that many of the hostilities aroused in everyday life are internalized within the body of the hostile person. The data mobilized by sociosomatic (psychosomatic) medicine give abundant confirmation to this statement. Hence the conclusion emerges that physical illness can, to an unknown extent, protect the social system against initiatives that might change it. The same point applies to some other forms of illness, such as immobilizing psychoneuroses or psychoses. When the incidence of such disabilities is kept within (unknown) limits, the effect is catharsis. It has often been observed in factories in the Soviet Union, as well as in the United States, that absences from work on health grounds frequently correlate sharply with deprivational changes in the factory situation, such as intense speedup or police repression.

Hostilities can also be in part discharged by morbid reveries, whether in the form of imagined disasters to the boss, or lugubrious fantasies about the self. Another example of internalized response is sluggish indifference to the environment, reflected in the desire for sleep and more sleep, or perpetual "loafing" around. Consolation may be sought in drug addiction, including alcohol; or in "escapist" literature, or solitary rambles. In the most extreme instances, we have total withdrawal from civilization into the life of a hermit, or suicide.

In addition to individual (ego) forms of internalization of the type just mentioned, many joint activities perform a catharsis function, lowering the hostility level of those who participate. Outstanding is sociability, whether "just to be with somebody" or for more positive conviviality. It is one province of talk, endless talk, to support the buffeted ego by receiving and giving symbolic evidence of respect and affection. Self-esteem is enhanced by the applause received for a resounding denunciation of something or other, or by the glorification of some heroic and defiant figure.

Many of the activities that can be carried on in private can be continued in a situation where others are present. One may engage in perfunctory talk while carrying along a stream of private fantasy; or sink, from time to time, into comatose lethargy or sleep. When the sociability includes sexual activity, sexual play and the orgasm are relied upon to provide that miscellaneous discharge of accumulated hostility that keeps many people going. It is a commonplace observation in daily life, to say nothing of the clinic, that hostilities often give rise to exaggerated demands for fondling (and other forms of tenderness) and for indulgence in all sorts of cranky food habits, or whims in arranging furniture and other details of the physical environment. Athleticism, which can be carried on privately or jointly, is another way of reducing tension by pushing a ball, a boxing partner or one's self.

The solemn rituals of society often dissipate waves of hostility and leave the social system intact. The distraught hang on the words of public worship; or, more properly, they cling to the total setting in which ceremonial (repetitive) patterns of religious observance are carried out. The situation provides symbolic scapegoats and saviors, to say nothing of opportunities for the combining of private autism with sociality.

Our own civilization has perfected new devices by which many catharsis functions are performed. One of the most remarkable devices is that of inducing people to sit in a darkened room and look at a blank wall on which a procession of shadows (accompanied by noise and music) appear. Although these shadow boxes (motion-picture theaters) permit autistic processes to continue in a sociable setting, the rush and boldness of the film sequence subjects the private reveries of the audience to some discipline.

Our civilization has worked out other ways of inducing large numbers of people to sit comparatively still and work off their hostilities. One is the spectator sports, like football or baseball, where after sitting (or standing) for a considerable period on a moving plank propelled by a gas or electric motor, great masses of people can again sit down while a limited number of vigorous young people attempt to interfere in permissible ways with one another's efforts to hit or carry a small object from one place to another. The people then disperse by sitting down again while they are carried back where they came from.

A great many joint activities that are called political and that evolve programs for changing the social system, in fact perform a catharsis function, since little comes of the program save some reduction of tension among the participants. (13) This was true of many political movements generated in this country in response to the business collapse of 1929. Some movements made use of world revolutionary symbols borrowed from communism, or were run by the Third International from outside the country. Others were inspired by the symbols invented outside the country for fighting against world communism, or were themselves run from outside the national boundaries. In addition, symbols were continued from previous American tradition, or were freshly invented (like "technocracy"); and there were native leaders of protest movements who had no organized tie with foreign organizations. Washington was besought to aid the bankers, manufacturers, merchants, executives, the skilled, the unskilled, students, farmers—indeed, all sections of our people. The measures actually adopted modified the previous practices of American life, but the basic structure of private ownership of the instruments of production, for example, survived; and no totalitarian dictatorship was installed. It is no exaggeration to say that one of the principal functions performed by the political organizations that sprang into existence during the depression was that of catharsis. The upshot was actually to bring about the adoption of policies that preserved the principal features of American society intact, though adapting in details to some transformations that were already far advanced before the crisis came. For millions of participants the meetings, demonstrations, petitions, publications and informal activities of these protest movements were a renewal of self-respect. Sufferers from bankruptcy and joblessness formed communes of mutual respect in which reciprocal acts of deference compensated in part for the hammer blows of economic fate.

But catharsis is not enough. We do not want to protect democracy by manipulating the community into a variety of activities deliberately encouraged or designed for the purpose of preserving as much of the status quo as possible. Any status quo deserves rational, selective, progressive change. We want a social equilibrium in which men receive the intelligence which they need for the making of rational choices, and in which they possess the skill and the will to make decisions that foster the free society. The aim is a continuing process of readjustment of prevailing institutions in a direction that more efficiently serves the ends of democracy. Within the framework of shared power, we require a decision-making process that actually does come up with the adjustments that maintain democratic unity of aim and act. We know that even an adequate stream of intelligence may not be used for rational purposes if the users are suffering from the tensions of sudden or accumulated destructiveness. Our task is to perfect both the intelligence function and the conditions that contribute the skill and motive adequate to the rational use of information. During the great depression, millions of men were made nonrational from want and humiliation. They were often in the mood to wreak havoc on everything in which they had formerly had faith. Under these circumstances the decisions made are likely to be so deformed by the pressure of destructive impulses that democracy or near-democracy can be destroyed in the process.

In a despotism, of course, catharsis is a major instrumentality of rule, and it has been carried to near-perfection in many despotic states for varying periods of time.

LAYMEN CHOOSE PHYSICIANS AND POLITICIANS

The task that confronts the policy scientist is parallel to that with which the physician has already had experience in dealing with lay citizens in a society where medical care is largely optional. In collective policy as in somatic medicine the problem is to improve the layman's judgment in selecting expert advisers and guides. It is no news that the layman is often the victim of misplaced confidence in choosing his physician and politician. There is a never-ending contest among those persons who believe themselves qualified to perform the functions of the physician or leader. Although the individual practitioner is not supposed to advertise, physicians as a group have long since learned to act jointly in order to protect themselves and the community at large from persons who represent themselves as ready and willing to perform the functions of the physician, but whom the profession holds to be unqualified. Medical associations use persuasion, propaganda, education, diplomacy (and similar means of political action) for such purposes. (14) The coercive facilities of the community have been influenced to set up and guarantee a licensing system, and therefore to sanction certain standards of education and procedure for the demonstration of competence. Today it is common for medical associations to take positive measures intended to enlighten the public about disease and health, and in this way to improve the layman's care of himself and choice of physician. It has become commonplace that unless the whole level of education is raised, many members of the community will succumb to the lure (and often to the malpractice) of impostors.

Those who want to practice social psychiatry or fulfill any other of the functions appropriate to the policy scientists of democracy have the practical problem of winning lay confidence in their good intentions and ability. In the first instance the task is to increase the number of men and women in the community, in places powerful or humble, who turn for understanding to properly qualified policy scientists. At present our civilization is not equipped with a public image of the practitioner of the sciences of democracy. This lack corresponds to the actual facts of society: There is no one professionally trained group that fully shares the goals and skills required by the effective democratic leader. Few of the professions concerned with society have created a public symbol. There is no unified figure of the "social scientist" who can be recognized (even in the cartoon strips). The psychiatrist has suffered from rather too much prominence in the films, where he often figures as a foreigner with dubious English whose stupidity is compounded with unmistakable symptoms of paranoia. Perhaps the "economist" comes close to providing a symbol that stands for some degree of special competence in describing certain collective features of our common life. But even the economist has not yet jelled into a readily identifiable symbol in the mass media of communication, which shows that he has not yet become part of our popular culture. The physician who is mainly concerned with public health and preventive medicine is also so recent that when, in a film or magazine article, you want to establish the professional status of such a person it is necessary to have the inevitable white coat and a test tube somewhere in the picture. As for the symbol "political scientist" or "professional student of government," there is almost no public image. So little, in fact, that Harold J. Laski and other members of the London School of Economics and Political Science find it convenient, on most occasions, to forget about the "political science" and call themselves economists (not always to the satisfaction of the matured-in-wood economists). As for sociologists, there is no visual image that has won general support, although ingenious and sometimes diabolical gentlemen often manage to convey the idea that sociologists are among the lunatic fringe, perilously near to being "socialists." In some ways the nearest comprehensive stereotype is "professor" (in the sense of academic figures who have had their fare paid to Washington) or "brain truster." And the image is often concocted from those quaint articles of infrequent and slow-footed solemnity, the academic cap, hood and gown.

THE LAWYER

There is, of course, the lawyer. Any physician who contemplates the possible scope of social psychiatry and finds that it corresponds in large part with the understanding and guidance of public policy may wonder whether the job has not been pre-empted in large part by the lawyers. After all, lawyers as well as physicians share the heavy dignity that comes of long acceptance. Side by side, these two professions have had their ups and downs in the history of most of the countries with which we are acquainted; and one can, without putting too much elastic into the definition, find lawyers and physicians in a very large number, at least, of the folk cultures of whom the ethnologists have some trace.

The fact is that lawyers have been trained for but a fraction of the task of the policy scientist or the informed leader of democracy. Whether trained for the job or not, nevertheless they often get it. The conventional law school turns out a specialist on predicting how an appellate court will respond if a controversy is put up to it. Without much exaggeration we can say that the distinctive core of the lawyer's skill is guessing about, and presenting cases to, courts. The attorney does not traditionally approach his client's problem by considering the impact upon the community of the alternative policies that confront the client. The lawyer focuses almost exclusively upon the job of pre-guessing the courts and deciding what would happen to the language of a given contractual, testamentary or other document if someone should, at a future time, under any imaginable circumstance, invoke the language before a court. If the lawyer becomes a judge of a lower tribunal, he continues to apply his accustomed criteria, since in the lower court he must bear in mind the probable behavior of the court of appeal (which under our system may mean the Supreme Court). If the lawyer is put on the bench of the Supreme Court, or any court of last resort, he is left rudderless, save that in choosing among the contentions put before him by counsel he is not insensitive to what his current colleagues will say or to what the courts of the future will say when they look back at his decision and opinion; or what professional opinion, which may eventually find expression in the courts, will be.

To say that the conventional training leaves the lawyer rudderless means that he is not made aware of the assumptions upon which he proceeds. He does not face up to the goal values that he himself prefers, or which are held with such and such a degree of unanimity in the community. Often the nearest approach to a goal value to be sought by the lawyer is "order." Does this mean that the only social result with which the lawyer is concerned is keeping down riots? If public order is understood in such police-court terms, it means that the value being pursued is the avoidance of situations in which people (and property) will be damaged or destroyed. To protect people from damage is the same value criterion as that of the physician. What the physician calls the "prevention and cure of disease" is called "the preservation of order" when the lawyer refers to the protection of life and limb.

In reality the lawyer does not limit himself to this strict interpretation of public order. He has an impact on the entire pattern of values and institutions. But he is not trained to think about these impacts or to relate them to a coherent and implicit set of assumptions about goal values, trends

and conditions. The usual training leaves him believing
that he has no opportunities or responsibilities other than
to serve his clients by whatever means are not forbidden.
And he moves in a world of perpetual self-congratulation in
which the glories of the law and hence of the lawyer are
suitable topics of declamation wherever the members of the
bar are ceremonially assembled.

Hence the usual training of the lawyer in our civilization
leaves him indoctrinated with a set of biases of the utmost
danger for democracy. The chief bias is that if he keeps himself and his client out of jail and out of undesired bankruptcy he is performing his full professional function. It is
assumed that in jousts among the knights of law, wearing
the favors of as many clients as possible, the maximum good
will automatically win. (15)

The assumption is true *only* where the competitors include vigorous and skillful protagonists of a comprehensive
positive conception of democratic policy. The trust in au-
tomatism is suspiciously like the faith proclaimed by Adam
Smith in the "Invisible Hand" that was supposed to enable
economic life to be carried on for the greatest benefit of all,
if everybody pursued his interest. The late Carl Becker
put the point with characteristic pungency when he described the ideology of liberal capitalism: "The impreg-
nable strength of nineteenth-century liberalism was chiefly
in this, that it recognized the high value of philanthropy
plus five percent: it united liberty and competition in the
holy bonds of wedlock, made liberty useful by setting it up
in business, and sanctified competition by anointing it with
the incense of human freedom." (16) Today, it cannot be
too often repeated; we have seen near-democracies fail because positive policies were too weak competitively to succeed. They did not get enough energy and ability mobilized

on their behalf, principally because energy and ability were
better rewarded for adding to the competitive strength of
(often unrecognized) destructive policies.

Although unequipped for enlightened leadership, lawyers continue to play an important part in the decision-
making process of modern life. They have succeeded in
consolidating their position by limiting judgeships to lawyers, and by establishing a licensing-examination system
to limit admissions to the bar. Hence it is not strictly true,
as Robert Louis Stevenson claimed, that "politics is perhaps
the only profession for which no preparation is thought
necessary." (17) More significant, perhaps, is the infiltration
of legally trained persons into many posts of advice and
decision, not only in the institutions called government, but
widely throughout society. Lawyers are essential in all major
policy-forming processes because they give expert guesses
about the damage that other lawyers (on the bench) may do
to what policy makers want to do. But they take no responsibility for analyzing the consequences of the advice they
give for the public order of democracy. Hence to the extent
that they are part of the destructive practices of our civilization, they can at least plead ignorance.

In what degree is the present legal profession having destructive consequences for democracy? Although this question has been raised by many lawyers and law teachers, well-
balanced and well-informed inquiries are few and far between. Is it true, for instance, that the weight of legal brains
is on the side of monopoly clients and that this undermines
the competitive system of free enterprise? (Monopolistic
business is a form of politics, and is called "business" by
mistake or design. One result of the mistake or design is
that the politicians who run monopoly business use the symbol "business" to obtain support from what remains of

genuinely competitive businessmen in the rivalry of monopoly-politicians with government-party-politicians.) Do the lawyers always make clear to their clients when the measures desired by the client undermine the American business system? For instance, that a given line of policy will probably contribute to the concentration of control over wealth and in this way endanger democratic institutions?

It may be urged, as it often is, that the lawyer is not sought by his client to give him lessons in democracy but to get results, regardless of what results, so long as they are not illegal. And furthermore, and everyone is entitled to his day in court, that this can be regarded as a basic respect requirement in a democratic society.

This does not, however, end the discussion. Most physicians recognize that in their professional capacity they serve not only the immediate minimum needs of a sufferer but the health needs of the community as well. Hence disease-breeding conditions in the environment are sought out, if not by the individual physician, at least through initiatives taken through his medical associations.

A professional association provides an instrument by which a division of labor can be organized which saves the individual physician from the carrying out of certain activities but enables him to get them going in the community. Precisely the same possibility exists for the bar associations. And to a certain degree the professional societies of the bar contribute to the clarifying of democratic policy. Associations of the bar have often supported the growth of new institutions whereby the poor are given more adequate defenders. Bar associations have often put through judicial reorganizations that were of benefit throughout society in the form of reduced costs of litigation and more speedy disposition of cases. The bar has often improved the personal honesty and ability of the bench by supporting only candidates who conformed to at least minimum standards.

The point of the present analysis is that there is grave reason to believe that the professional societies have kept their eyes averted from the most dangerous threats to our political and social ideals. It is not customary for bar associations to clarify and recommend policies that in their considered judgment, after proper inquiry, will enable our economy to operate at high levels of productive employment; or which measures can be taken to maintain a more vigorous free market sector in our economy; or what policies will, if private monopolies cannot be made competitive, make them more responsible.

NONLEGAL PROFESSIONS

Social psychiatrists are warranted in concluding that the lawyer, despite his degree of success in playing an active part in decision making, has not met the needs of democracy. But what of the other learned skills? Has the field been preempted by the clergy, the educators, the social scientists, or the physical scientists? Let me anticipate the result of the paragraphs that follow by saying that while each profession does a job that is in many ways admirable, no group gives the community the full benefit of its judgment in clarifying democratic policy, or has won the full confidence of the community as adviser or decision maker.

Consider what is perhaps the group whose impact has been most sensational on human welfare—the physical scientists and particularly the atomic physicists. The bombs dropped on Japanese civilians detonated a crisis of moral indignation in the lives of thousands of scientists who had assisted in one way or another in the creation of the new instrument of destruction. Many of them were under the

impression that the government had firmly promised to refrain from using the weapon unless the enemy was known
to be on the verge of introducing it. Or, if the enemy did
not discover the secret, it was believed that the government
would stage a demonstration and demand peace before killing men, women and children in a surprise attack on enemy
cities. Stricken by the havoc wrought by their brilliance,
these atomic scientists fumed against the military restrictions which at first prevented them from ventilating their
views on public policy, and then vehemently threw themselves into the struggle for civilian control. A small group
of vigorous leaders helped to defeat the proposals to place
the entire development under the control of military rather
than civil authorities. Next, they tried to work out globally
acceptable ideas about how to control the destructive application of nuclear energy, in the hope of turning this geyser
of physical power to the constructive service of humanity.
These men became policy-minded under the shock of the
blood that they could not wipe off their consciences. (18)

The fervent, and partially successful, exertions of the
atomic physicists have underlined the political indifference
of the large body of our fellow citizens who are allowed to
acquire and exercise scientific skill. From the physical scientists has come knowledge that has led to the drastic reconstruction of technology. But physical scientists have been
notoriously close to industries wealthy enough to employ
them and build suitable laboratories. Distinguished scientists have sometimes absorbed the partisan opinions of the
businessmen of their acquaintance without applying to social problems the same skeptical judgment and open awareness of postulates with which the scientist is accustomed to
proceed when he deals with physical nature.

At the same time, some physical scientists have openly

associated themselves with revolutionary and subversive movements, bitterly attacking their colleagues for subserviency to the ruling class of plutocracy. This is disturbing enough in itself to conservative and also to liberal opinion. And it is even more upsetting when it is disclosed that able scientists can be led into the betrayal of their country out of dissent from the policies of their government (as in Canada). (19)

In this state of social entanglement without comprehension, the physical scientists have been slow to discover themselves as full citizens of society. The professional associations of physical scientists have not organized policy commissions authorized to clarify the ends of democracy, or to enlighten either the members of the associations or the general community on the policies by which such goals can probably be attained. As with the medical or the law societies, it is entirely feasible for the working scientist, chiefly preoccupied with his laboratory or observatory, to entrust colleagues to look into these matters by seeking pertinent knowledge wherever and by whatever means are appropriate. From time to time reports can supply guidance on civil affairs. Obviously such guidance need not be accepted by the scientist or by the community. But it can be taken into account for what it is believed to be worth as the expression of a known group of persons of ascertainable traits and interests.

As for the social scientists (including the educators), they, too, do not fully answer the needs of democratic science or leadership. It is true that some social scientists play active and successful parts as advisers and decision makers. Political scientist Woodrow Wilson, sociologist William Graham Sumner, economist John Maynard Keynes are names that suggest the role taken by some of the more successful. The

Treasury and the Federal Reserve Banks have long been in rather close contact with economists. Sociologists and social psychologists have contributed to the policies of the Department of Agriculture. Political scientists are especially numerous in the Budget. Psychologists are found in the Civil Service Commission, and anthropologists have had an impact on the Indian Service (located in the Interior Department). Diplomatic historians have been drawn upon by the State Department (and in World War II they were especially numerous in the Research and Intelligence Branch of the Office of Strategic Services). Private industry has drawn increasingly upon all social-science specialties as they have developed, the most recent examples being sociologists and anthropologists who study social class relations (respect). Market research makes use of many of the techniques developed for the study of the process of communication in society. Churches have been influenced, especially in their rural programs, by community and regional studies.

Although the permeation of specialists on the social process into advisory posts, and even posts of final responsibility, has gone farther than is generally known, it is unquestionably correct to say that they have fallen short when appraised by the criteria we have applied to lawyers, physical scientists (and physicians). Several factors help to account for this unsatisfactory state of affairs. One is the conflict that results from the demand to achieve the same reputation, when they speak on social questions, that the physical scientist or the physician has when he speaks on physical science or medicine. Economists, political scientists, sociologists and their colleagues are only too well aware that the layman is utterly confused about whose word is most likely to be true about human relations. Many social scientists have deliberately sought to extricate themselves from the moralizing traditions of the social reformers and to devote themselves to expanding the boundaries of knowledge about human affairs. To do this they have concerned themselves with method, as we mentioned before, and glorified abstinence from any comprehensive perspective over the policy problems of democracy. The more scholarly members of the profession have recalled the role that was played by the University of Leyden, for instance, toward the close of the wars of religion in Europe, when scholars deliberately turned their back on religious and political polemics and sought a more fundamental grasp of the processes of man and nature. (20)

They have also reflected on the lowly estate of the physical sciences until the great outburst of the sixteenth century and since. It has often been pointed out that no sooner did Galileo formulate certain laws of motion than Thomas Hobbes instantly called for a science of man that would reduce human relations, too, to "motions." Every advance in the probing of physical configurations has led at once by extrapolation to calls for a science of man paralleling the conceptions and procedures current in dealing with physical events. Books have frequently been written, for instance, that purport to provide a prolegomenon for the social sciences. A favorite device is to apply the calculus of variations and to enumerate a list of terms which are then manipulated in a variety of equations. (21) Frequently there are no operational indexes for the terms, and the entire enterprise turns out to be an exercise in substituting in equations serviceable in some field of physical science a notational system that is unrelated to any observations made about social processes. The making of such pseudo-contributions and the elaborate efflorescence from time to time of imaginative "systems" have led some critical minds to the view that the study of human relations is so immature that many generations will pass before any dependable basis will be found for descriptive propositions about social equilibrium. (22)

Such factors have made for the withdrawal by many able specialists from any attempt to encourage the clarifying of democratic goal values or to make available to the public comprehensive analyses of the alternative lines of policy by which such values can probably be achieved. Some social scientists have sought to limit themselves to the detailed investigation of very limited configurations wherein the physical sciences, as understood by the social scientist, could be most carefully imitated. (23)

Many of the social scientists who have become policy advisers have attempted to reduce the vulnerability of their position against claims of partisanship by stressing their "neutrality." This applies particularly to civil servants engaged in what is called public management or administration. The contention is that there is a special complex of skills that apply to the conduct of activities in far-flung administrative services, such as the vast departments and agencies of government. It is argued that democracies as well as despotisms need experts. And the expert will only be accepted as such if he is careful to preserve his "neutrality."

A reputation for neutrality can be gained by abstaining from many of the practices urged upon the active citizen by traditional democratic theory. According to the tradition, the citizen is obligated not only to vote, but to speak up for what he approves of. The man who inhibits his opinion on grounds of expediency is therefore falling short of his civic duty. In justification of the neutrality of the civil servant, the argument is that the execution of the policy laid down by the legislature and the chief executive calls for a corps of officials who are sufficiently well disciplined to put the policy into effect, regardless of private preferences. Otherwise, efficient administration cannot be obtained, since the policy of each step will be re-argued at every link of the chain of execution.

It is further contended that the official must, in order to preserve the neutrality essential to efficiency, abstain from public criticism of the policy or from the support of alternative policies. The outspokenness of the civil servant is therefore curbed in the expectation that, on balance, democracy has more to gain by efficient execution than from anything the public administrators might contribute to public discussion.

With the enormous growth of the public services in modern states, however, manifest dangers to democracy appear if the demand for neutrality results in the enforcement of silence upon ever-widening groups in the community. If the man on a government payroll can vote only in secret, he is partly disenfranchised, and if most of the community is in government employ, for instance, the legislative process (the top decision-making procedure) is left to the minority. More and more members of the community become half-citizens, and an atmosphere of timidity enhances the traditional characteristics that have transformed so many officials into "bureaucrats." In a socialist community, the rigid enforcement of neutrality might very well leave top policy in the hands of a tiny fraction.

Perhaps a partial solution of the difficulty is to be found in allowing "neutrality" on the part of the individual official while insisting upon active contributions through authorized professional associations. As in the case of the bar association or the medical society, commissions and staffs can study and report both to members and the community at large. In addition to reports that bear on special fields of interest, each association can deal with the entire range of questions involved in goal statement, alternative-analysis and recommendation. Whatever risks are involved in under-mining confidence in impartiality are less than the risk of disenfranchising elements in society who can make useful direct contributions to the opinion-forming process, and who can be prevented from relapsing into the timidity of half-citizens afraid "to stick their necks out." It is incom-patible with democracy to allow the "passion for anonym-ity" to degenerate into a passion for quiet job holding by citizen-castrates.

The upshot of our analysis can be expressed in these con-clusions: Democratic leadership is a key problem of the as yet poorly developed policy sciences of democracy. The problem of leadership, on examination, proves to be equiv-alent to the task of understanding how to bring the entire community to the level of equilibrium that sustains democ-racy. The issue is society-wide because the elite of democracy includes all levels of the community. The democratic equi-librium is one in which human destructiveness, whether of impulse or practice, is kept low. Hence it appears that the problem of democratic leadership and eliteship is equiv-alent to the development of social health rather than disease. This appears to be the program of social psychiatry, in par-ticular, among the medical sciences. Hence social psychiatry becomes equivalent in scope to the policy sciences of democ-racy, the sciences which discover the factors that condition the democratic equilibrium. As the policy sciences are de-veloped, they must succeed in winning the confidence of the lay community which, in a free society, chooses leaders and physicians. To some extent leaders are selected today from professionally qualified persons, notably lawyers. But con-ventional legal training does not equip the lawyer, even when successfully participating in the decision-making processes, to apply the policy sciences. The needed point of view is missing from his equipment and conception of his role. The same point applies to the other professions having an obvious impact on policy, such as the physical and social sciences. These groups do not make full use of their professional associations to supplement what the individual expert is able to do in contact with his patient or client. By developing commissions and staffs through its organization, every profession can seek to clarify the aims, conditions and policy alternatives of democracy, both to its members and to the community at large. In this way the policy sciences can extend their usefulness in the decision-making process of society.

VII. THE FORMATION OF
DEMOCRATIC PERSONALITY

THE PROGRESSIVE democratization of society calls for the amending of social institutions for the purpose of aiding the development of democratic personality and of providing for a decision-making process that fulfills the goal values of a democratic commonwealth. If the policy sciences are to aid democracy, they must contribute to the continual reconstruction of whatever practices stand in the way of democratic personality and polity.

These principles phrase in action form the inferences that spring from the analyses made in preceding chapters. We have emphasized the fact that democratic leadership does not depend upon specialized training of the few so much as upon elevating the level of the entire democratic elite, which embraces the whole community. Our analysis of human destructiveness called attention to the interpersonal context which embraces both impulses and practices. And this, it will be remembered, is substantially equivalent to the problem of health and disease in society.

We also phrased the democratic problem in terms of interacting value variables. The goal variables, shared power and respect, reinforce one another, and in turn can be supported by a proper relation to other value variables in the equilibrium of society. They are dependent upon the sharing of enlightenment—a point that is not only scientifically tenable but is a standard plank of democratic doctrine and of the United States Constitution. As Justice Black phrased it recently, in reference to the First Amendment: "That Amendment rests on the assumption that the widest possible dissemination of information from diverse and antagonistic sources is essential to the welfare of the public." (1)

That shared power and respect (and enlightenment) depend upon a very considerable dispersion of wealth throughout the community is a maxim of political science whose origins are lost in classical times. The point was stated in 1919 by the late Professor Irving Fisher with characteristic vigor: "Our society will always remain an unstable and explosive compound as long as political power is vested in the masses and economic power in the classes. In the end one of these powers will rule. Either the plutocracy will buy up the democracy or the democracy will vote away the plutocracy." (2)

Any pattern of values that is not supported by shared conceptions of moral approval (rectitude) is in that degree unstable. The function of the doctrines comprising the political myth of democracy is to evoke and crystallize moral sentiment in favor of democracy as against another form of government and society. As Mosca, in common with all systematic political thinkers, has pointed out, though the doctrines of a community are not necessarily to be taken as scientific hypotheses or laws, they "answer a real need in man's social nature; and this need, so universally felt, of knowing that one is governed not on the basis of mere material or intellectual force, but on the basis of a moral principle, has beyond any doubt a practical and real importance." (3)

The stability of a democratic community undoubtedly depends upon the formation of characters capable of respecting the basic humanity of all men. The sharing of power and respect in adult life depends, in no small part, on basic character structure (which we have classified as part of well-being, along with somatic integrity). This is consistent with part, at least, of William Penn's famous overstatement: "If men be good, government cannot be bad." (4) Penn also was referring to the interlocking bonds of affection that give strength to social structure.

DEMOCRATIC PERSONALITY

The basic conception of personality is that of characteristic ways in which a person responds to people. We might describe personality in terms of temperament, character, attitude, functional type or role. In our discussion of democratic personality the principal emphasis is upon character, functional type and role, with temperament and aptitude entering into the picture when they account for the first three.

The fully developed citizen of a democratic commonwealth will willingly and skillfully play at least certain minimum roles. He will share the perspectives of democratic doctrine, which, as we have had occasion to say, include positive identification with humanity (and with all smaller groups whose activities are consistent with the larger whole); demands for a society where within the framework of shared power and respect all values are made more abundant and available; and expectations that men *can* do on a universal and permanent scale what they have so often accomplished on a more local and temporary scale. Besides these doctrinal perspectives, the citizen will maintain some degree of active and informed participation in public affairs. This calls for a basic equipment of skills of thought, observation and social manipulation. Under intercrisis conditions, the citizen's minimum may go only so far as keeping an eye on community developments, perhaps acting through professional and occupational associations, in addition to civic or party organizations, to receive reports on the facts and to clarify objectives of policy.

All this coincides with the traditional conception of the active and responsible citizen of a free society in which power, though taken seriously, is subordinated to the value goals of human dignity and the abundant commonwealth. Despite the ups and downs of American public life since the adoption of the Constitution, we know that a very considerable element has taken politics seriously, agreeing with Cato (Governor George Clinton), writing in 1787, that the "disposal of your reputation, and of your lives and property, is more momentous than a contract or a farm, or the sale of a bale of goods." (5)

But we cannot wisely ignore the fact that there are and have been abundant signs of depolitical, apolitical and antipolitical attitudes. When there has been a decrease in politicization of a person's conduct due to disillusionment with power as a value, or with the power process, we speak of him as depolitical. When disinterest in power results from its depreciation as compared with the enhanced value of other practices, such as science and art, we speak of an apolitical person. When participation in the power process is actively opposed on the grounds of its alleged incompatibility with other values, we have to do with the antipolitical person, who, for instance, may be a religious mystic concerned with rectitude, a scientist concerned with skill in discovering truth or a snob who is discomfited by the "mob." (The latter attitude was expressed by Washington Irving: "I am as deep in mud and politics as ever a modern gentleman would wish to be; and I drank beer with the multitude; and I talked hand-bill fashion with the demagogues; and I shook hands with the mob, whom my heart abhorreth. . . . Truly this saving one's country is a nauseous piece of business, and if patriotism is such a dirty virtue,—prythee, no more of it.") (6)

Our special concern at the moment is for the character component of basic democratic personality. We know that there can be nondemocrats from lack of exposure to the doctrines and techniques of democracy. But we are especially interested in the non- or antidemocrats who have rejected democracy after being extensively exposed to it, or who imagine that they conform to the democratic ideal when they are undemocratic in actual conduct.

Our aim is to bring into being democratic leaders who share the basic personality structure appropriate to the elite of a society where power is subordinated to respect and to identifications with humanity. The chief difference between the "basic" citizen and the democratic leader needs to be mainly a difference of skill and not of values.

In any case the development of democratic personality involves the fundamental process of displacing motivations first organized in the primary circle upon the larger environment, and their legitimation in terms of the public good.

FAILURE THROUGH NONIDENTIFICATION

As a reminder of the deviations from democratic personality development that frequently occur among us, I propose to recite briefly from the history of a successful physician. His first active participation in political life came during the depression when he gave covert financial support to a group of reserve army officers who were concerned with the threat of communism, and who brought him in contact with Americans who were working with Italian fascists and German nazis, who were regarded as bulwarks against revolution. Dr. B had nothing to say about the excesses of the Italians or the Germans, focusing his hatred entirely against Russia. Having become a financial angel, the physician was drawn more and more into the company of Russian émigré conspirators, and also began to look around for an American politician who would do for our "degenerate" country what Il Duce and the Fuehrer had done elsewhere.

What was behind this development? Dr. B came from the family of a small-town businessman. His mother was from a wealthier and better-established family, and was insistent that her son go into law or medicine. From his mother, B acquired a faintly condescending attitude toward his father. He took an unusually severe medical course and became a highly specialized scientist and practitioner. He felt that the choice of his profession was not entirely his own, but he swallowed his resentment against the pressure that had been put on him. Several other choices were practically made for him in the same way, including his marriage.

At school B subjected himself to a strenuous grind, taking it much harder than most of his fellow students. He was censorious of all who did not drive themselves as much as he did, and felt that he had sacrificed so much that he deserved every honor and opportunity that came his way. In connection with internship and charity work he was in touch with types of humanity who differed enormously from those in his home town, where there were no Negroes and no immigrants from Central and Southern Europe, and no Catholics or Jews. He felt contempt rather than sympathy for the alcoholics, prostitutes, addicts, dope peddlers and others with whom he came in contact. His academic specialty led him to stress the importance of inborn factors as the determiner of what he called "sound human stuff," of which he believed there was very little.

Dr. B not only felt infinitely superior to the flotsam and jetsam of the community whom he served at the charity hospital, but he felt no less resentment toward the alleged slackness of the city institutions with which he came in contact. He resented the bowing and scraping to the politicians, and cultivated the acquaintance of a circle of affluent patients with whom he was building up a lucrative private practice in his specialty.

Without at the moment delving deeply into the inner structure of the doctor's personality, two or three points stand out. He made few identifications with other people. There was some rigid, limiting process at work that led him to deal with stereotypes of race, nationality, income or social class, and kept him uniformly distant from and contemptuous of the "underdog." Dr. B's exposure to democratic tradition was quite ample, and yet his character structure functioned as a selective antidemocratic predisposition.

Note, too, the paradoxical nature of B's rejection of democracy. He was himself a striking instance of the person who is provided with ample opportunities to rise in a highly mobile society; yet he accumulated so much destructive hostility in the process of growing up and mastering a profession that he came to reject some of the leading features of the society from which he benefited.

FAILURE THROUGH DISILLUSIONMENT

The second brief case excerpt concerns a brilliant journalist who while making his living as a professional friend of the people had the utmost loathing for the doctrines of democracy and the institutions of this or any country that professed respect for men in the mass. Aside from his private vituperativeness C engaged in few overtly antidemocratic activities. However, he was always on the watch for the great leader who he imagined would some day appear to put an end to all the corruption that he imagined was everywhere around. Often C would develop a prodigious enthusiasm for some new public figure, especially if he was "tough" and "hard boiled." Although as an adolescent C had flirted with all the political "isms" and at least two religious cults, he made a rather shamefaced private conversion to a church whose hierarchical organization seemed to him free of democratic sentimentality, and whose policies he believed made no concessions to mass ignorance, pettiness and "apathy with occasional fits of madness."

C grew up in the family of a schoolteacher and, despite some worries about his physique, took a vigorous and successful part in intellectual and social life. Around adolescence he became exceedingly disappointed in his father and presently left home, failed to go ahead with any systematic education and, after a great deal of bumming around, gravitated into journalism. His sarcastic literary style paved the way for great success, much of which was in crusades. He exposed all sorts of scandals and became something of a specialist in uncovering abuses of power.

One outstanding trait of C was a hard-boiled exterior and a soft-boiled interior. His sentimentality came out in the tender human-interest stories that he wrote about orphans and stray dogs, and in the special gift funds which he initiated for a "hard luck" cripple, or for "saving" someone from a mental institution where he had allegedly been "railroaded." At no time did C discover any general view of the social process or arrive at any coherent picture of the trends or problems of his time.

In talking to old friends C often said that the break with his father came from a sudden realization that his father was a bad example, having frittered away his excellent native talents on the trifling job of being a schoolmaster. But in more intimate circumstances (when C was being treated for alcoholism) it turned out that the break with the father had a different basis. C imagined that he had come upon his father one day in the school building making love to another teacher. Actually the father denied this, and tried to explain to the youth that he was exaggerating a trivial and innocent incident. But the boy stuck obstinately and morosely to his "disillusionment," feeling that his whole world had fallen to pieces. C believed that his mother was being betrayed and that his father was a pious fraud.

Actually the deep dependency demands in C's personality accounted for the shock. Although he continued to displace his hostilities upon all sorts of authorities, there was also another attitude, a continual search for some idea or person whom he could depend on entirely, trust implicitly.

THE GROWTH OF POLITICAL IMAGES

These case fragments call attention to the usefulness of being informed in detail about the growth of political images in the development of young people of all cultures, classes and periods of crisis or intercrisis. During any given period a culture (and a given position in a culture) provides a characteristic sequence of primary circles to which infants, children and young people are exposed. In addition, the culture supplies a characteristic sequence of exposure to symbols of reference to the secondary circles of society (the environment beyond the primary circle). Both the primary circle and the secondary symbols, therefore, are brought to the focus of attention in a discoverable pattern. Obviously the secondary symbols (as well as the symbols of reference to the primary circle) acquire meanings to the child in accord with the contexts in which they occur. Hence they are at hand for the displacement of affects from the immediate circle.

Images of the secondary environment acquire meanings (which may also be standard for a similarly situated group) by direct *extension* or by *compensation*. One of the questions for which data are not now at hand is whether political images acquire their meanings primarily by one or the other process at any given time and place. If we are to understand the growth of democratic personality, such facts as the following are needed:

Is the image of the good mother smoothly projected upon the mother country, if the country is presented as a woman symbol? Is the image of a bad mother (or father) extended to the country when it is symbolized as the fatherland? Are disappointments in the demands made upon the primary circle compensated by displacing the demands upon a remote and ever-indulgent image? Or, on the contrary, are the disappointments extended to cover even remote images, so that the entire world of authority becomes peopled with austere, depriving figures? Do the names of political parties, racial and religious groups, nations and other collective symbols of identification become defined as extensions of a good or bad father, grandfather, mother, grandmother, older or younger sibling figure? Or, on the contrary, do they grow into compensating images?

It is worth inquiring more fully into the precise structure of political images as they are developed in the early experience of the child. To what extent are the images shaped into *indulging or depriving figures in relation to specific values?* In more detail: The president or general or pope may appear as a threat of chastisement or annihilation, or as a defender against being bullied by parents, brothers and playmates. The secondary figure can be big and strong and well, and capable of making one big, strong and well, or little, puny and sick. Perhaps the political image is portrayed as a giver or depriver of candy and other good things to eat. The emphasis may be on giving or receiving affection in the form of fondling the body. Perhaps the secondary image is a dispenser or withholder of applause at one's prowess in climbing or running. Or the secondary image is a formidable source of scowls and moral condemnation, or of approval for "being good." Or the political symbol is elaborated as a teacher of skills, aiding one to shoot more expertly, or to ride or dance. Possibly the secondary figure has great secret knowledge. (Thus expectations and demands are patterned in relation to such values as power, well-being, wealth, affection, respect, rectitude, skill, enlightenment.)

The image of the secondary environment is elaborated further, by extension or compensation, according to the *conditions under which they give indulgence or impose deprivation.* Among these expectations about the conditions, the most important are the acts that are supposed to bring about the indulgence or obviate the deprivation. Perhaps it is assumed that results can only be obtained by overpowering the secondary image with the aid of others. It may be that physical pain must be endured to obtain satisfaction. Or a material gift must be offered. Perhaps a declaration of love will suffice. Or a very elaborate rigamarole must be undergone in which the maker of a request subjects himself to much self-abasement. Or the claim is established by the performing of many good deeds. Or the essential point is the skillful execution of some operation. Or secret knowledge must be demonstrated. (These images outline the scope for which various base values can be used in relation to authority.)

The secondary figures may be shown as arbitrary and unreasonable, or as amenable to the application of knowable rules. Furthermore, the figures can be arranged in strict hierarchical order, left in a scattered and unworked-out relation, or given a coarchical status (of equality). The images can be kept distinct or blended with figures that refer to extranatural personifications or forces. The president or the king may be blended with sun and light, and supplied with a halo.

A secondary image, once given shape, can be incorporated through identification in the self of the child, perhaps passing through several phases of incorporation and exclusion. In the child's early role-playing he becomes the sun, god, general, or president, and invokes the enlarged self in relation to other secondary images, or to the primary circle. (Even in relation to the primary circle the enlarged self may not be put fully to the test, since the demand on the immediately present person may be made in imagination.)

TACTICS IN THE PRIMARY CIRCLE

In evaluating the significance of the various processes of displacement for the evolution of the democratic personality, we must not lose sight of the tactics of direct action which are tried out in the primary circle as a means of obtaining direct indulgence and avoiding deprivation. It is possible and convenient to differentiate the observed tactics according to the value classification with which we have been working. If some acts are interfered with, the infant or child reacts with all the means at his disposal for inflicting deprivations upon the environment. And if acts are gratified, the response given to the environment may use the total repertory available at the stage of growth (such as the smile).

When acts are interfered with, and the result is to set off a storm of response, the infant-child is responding "totally" by the use of the most extreme measures at his command. Joan Riviere has written the most graphic account of the aggressions with which the child is overwhelmed and against which he tries to protect himself. "The child is overwhelmed by choking and suffocating; its eyes are blinded with tears, its ears deafened, its throat sore; its bowels gripe, its evacuations burn! (7) Such surging inner impulses precipitate what Freud called 'fear of the instincts.' " (8) In a sense, therefore, the infant-child begins by using "political" means, and only gradually learns to save for emergency use some of the most drastic responses open to him. We have defined the basic power relation as that in which extreme deprivations are threatened or inflicted against a challenger; and what the infant-child does initially is to treat every discomfort as a provocation for every form of expression at his command. *It is not too far fetched to say that everyone is born a politician, and most of us outgrow it.* In a society where extreme deprivations are provoked or used by no one, the outgrowing would be complete.

It is no simple matter to decide what forms of expression in any situation are democratic. We can, of course, settle all questions by definition. But which definition? Often we need careful data of observation before we can decide whether certain patterns of conduct do, or do not, affect the levels of conduct about which we have no hesitation in using the term democratic. Take the simple question whether a child shall be permitted to address his parents by the first name. I don't need to remind you how scandalized some parents are at the practice, although they believe themselves to be genuine democrats and agree that they do not want to build up useless or destructive barriers between young and old or strong and weak. I doubt whether we have enough specific information at hand today to demonstrate what difference, if any, it makes one way or the other.

Another example is what we are to call permissible assertiveness and impermissible aggression. There is not much difficulty in reference to dramatic cases of physical violence, but there is much uncertainty about intermediate conduct. And this is accentuated by the circumstance that much of our existing literature on self-assertion leaves out the vocal pattern. Scientific work on the problem has been held back by the clumsy gadgets that have been available for recording and reproducing the voice in action in concrete life situations. It has been exceedingly difficult to make clear from one situation to the next what intonations are called threatening, commanding, requesting and the like. (9)

THE SOCIAL-ANXIETY HYPOTHESIS

As we examine the growth of political images relating to the remote environment and of tactical responses to the primary circle, one major hypothesis stands out for investigation from the standpoint of democratic personality development. Stated in many ways by many scientists, exemplified by data obtained by many procedures of observation, this hypothesis has gradually taken the center of the stage. In this context I shall call it the "social-anxiety hypothesis." The conception is that personality failure is often a failure of basic character formation, and that defective character is a function of *interpersonal situations in which low estimates of the self are permitted to develop.*

The hypothesis emphasizes the point that the devaluation of the self is in terms of the evaluations of other persons. From low self-estimates come a host of defensive reactions, running the gamut from hopeless acquiescence to reaction formations (and other compensatory devices). These destructive processes imperil the potentialities of the person to enter into a fully creative and congenial relationship with others. When such relations are achieved in the primary circle, it may be at the cost of the wider environment, since destructive demands that are held in check in the face-to-face situation may be expressed in the acceptance of such paranoidlike conceptions as the myth of a uniquely chosen people or of an "inevitable" revolutionary triumph or of an alleged revelation of the full truth (to be compared with the partial truth of others).

Social anxiety, therefore, is acute concern for the *deference* responses of others, and includes the incorporation and application to the self of deprivational appraisals. We have spoken of differentiations of deference in terms of values such as affection, respect, rectitude and power. The *welfare* values include well-being, in the sense of safety and bodily integrity, wealth, including consumption materials, skill and enlightenment; and these appear to affect character formation only when they become involved in deference responses. According to the social-anxiety hypothesis democratic character develops only in those who esteem themselves enough to esteem others (to use a phrase of Harry Stack Sullivan's). (10) The newborn member of society must receive enough positive indulgence from the human environment to enable him to be indulgent toward himself and others. Such a basic character formation operates selectively as an enduring predisposition in subsequent life situations. It makes it possible for the person to supply himself with indulgence in circumstances in which a favorable ratio of indulgence is not accorded to prodemocratic conduct by the environment. This is the basis for the extraordinary capacity of some human beings to remain generous, warm, enduring, hopeful and spontaneous when others project blame, dash themselves to pieces or retire, trailing clouds of regressive fantasy. Democratic characters have a durable positive image of the potentialities of human nature.

DESPOTISM AND LOW ESTIMATES OF SELF

The most drastic form of the social-anxiety hypothesis applied to politics is that *men can only be free when they are free of social anxiety*. The appearance of a tyrant is an extreme sign of mass demands for the devalued self to depend upon someone else. So long as these dependency demands are generated in the lives of men, the masses will force themselves upon potential tyrants, even though at first glance it looks as though the tyrants were forcing themselves on the masses.

Were men free, so runs the hypothesis, they would instantly protect themselves against the attempt of anyone to reduce them to dependence. Confronted by superior physical strength, the free man will promptly obtain allies and check the bully-tyrant. Not only must the tyrant sleep, as Hobbes said, but combinations of the weak can check and overcome the strong, a point which is gracefully put in the wisdom of the *Panchatantra:*

> Woodpecker and sparrow
> With froggy and gnat,

Attacking *en masse,* laid
The elephant flat. (11)

Most disturbing of all the consequences of anxiety-induced unfreedom is the fact that rebellion is self-defeating. Even successful rebellion brings to the top a person who is strongly disposed to use his newly found strength to confirm his own freedom by renewing the chains of others. The rebel chief rises to power on a phalanx of slaves who substitute one golden image for the last, remaining as servile as before. Hence the cynicism of the proverb, "The more things change, the more they remain the same." On the disappointing results of revolution, Sorel wrote:

Experience has always shown us hitherto that revolutionaries plead "reasons of state" as soon as they get into power, that they employ police methods and look upon justice as a weapon which they may use unfairly against their enemies. (12)

This is the vicious-circle conception of politics, which when carried to its doctrinal conclusion is made articulate in statements like those of the Muslim commentator Jamâ'a in the fourteenth century, when the *Civitas Dei* aspiration of the Islamic world had failed:

The sovereign has a right to govern until another and stronger one shall oust him from power and rule in his stead. The latter will rule by the same title and will have to be acknowledged on the same grounds; for a government, however objectionable, is better than none at all; and between two evils we must choose the lesser. (13)

The social-anxiety hypothesis points to a way by which the vicious circle can be broken, and a spiral instead of a circle can be realized in practical life.

THE HYPOTHESIS OF SEXUAL-POLITICAL FREEDOM

From what specific sources comes the willingness of human beings to abdicate initiative and self-direction before some living image whom they inflate to supercolossal dimensions and bow down before? For an answer, it is suggested we must go not only to the fact of anxiety but to the specific tensions that have been acquired in the struggle to express native impulses in ways forbidden by authority. What are the impulses typically involved in this clash over permissible modes of expression? The *sexual,* states one hypothesis. The interference is accomplished by physical chastisement, by expostulation, by ridicule, by withdrawal of affection—in a word, by severe deprivations administered in every sphere of values. And if there is rage or persistence? This is met by greater deprivation until eventually the person resolves the difficulty by incorporating the taboo within the self, and thenceforth administers the command through the automatic experiencing of anxiety when the offending impulse is aroused to a significant degree.

The effects of crippled sexuality are far more pervasive on this theory than if they touched only the simple domain of physical activity. Restrictions, once imposed, radiate through the personality and place curbs of various degrees of severity on other forms of impulse, until the entire structure is permeated by conflict. The self-mutilating process can include the higher mental operations, so that the taboo on vigorous sexuality can damage the individual in his quest for knowledge. The curbs can be expressed in any authority situation, whether the person or official involved be foreman, policeman, teacher, judge or politician. Any person or any symbol is eligible to have displaced upon him or it the role of the potential inflictor of sanctions so serious that struggle is futile.

And the analysis goes further. Overcompensations can occur in which the anxieties of submission are partly defied by dashes into antiauthoritarianism. But this betrays its unhealthy origin in many ways, especially in the provoking of the environment into acts that gratify repressed guilt feelings. The revolt may be expressed and exhausted by making use of any one of the neurotic, psychopathic or psychotic manifestations with which psychiatry is so well acquainted. Defiance can even be expressed as sexual defiance, which can occur without dissipating much of the underlying anxiety. Hence the rebel remains a cripple, in this case ridden with specific preoccupations with sex and incapable of rising to the level of diversified and abundant expression of native energy and talent. In return for a limited and defiant exercise of physical sexuality, he relinquishes the possibilities of expressing himself to the full in relation to power, wealth, enlightenment and other values.

Rebelliousness can break out in all manner of active rather than neurotic expressions, such as provocative delinquency, gangsterism and tyrannization over everyone who can be beaten or intimidated into submission. The ascendancy (the "charisma") of many so-called natural leaders turns out to be that of the successful delinquent. No one can look at the psychological structure of the tyrannies of recent world politics without recognizing that such political leadership is juvenile delinquency on a colossal scale. In the immediate struggle for power, one set of delinquents fights it out with another set, and with one another individually; and the balance of power is tipped by the weight of the psychic-castrates whom the successful delinquent is able to intimidate into accepting him as a hero.

In a word, men are not born slaves but have slavery thrust upon them through interference with healthy sexual development. In partial support of the connection between despotism and frustrated sexuality, Wilhelm Reich, who is perhaps the most outspoken applier of the sexual hypothesis to politics, calls attention to the puritanical trends in the sexual policies of the Soviet Union. (14) As totalitarian tendencies gain the upper hand, the rulers of Russia reimpose all the hated forms of sexual frustration that were once pilloried as a device of capitalist exploitation.

Is the policy inference that sexual permissiveness and enlightenment are capable of preparing millions of oncoming adolescents for vigorous democratic citizenship? When the question is posed in this blunt fashion, it is often pointed out that we cannot be sure of the results if we begin by trying to change the standards of adolescent conduct. Adolescents, it is said, have already been warped by what has happened to their sexuality earlier in life, say during the fourth year. Suddenly enlarged sexual freedom at adolescence may precipitate acute crises of "transition." (Orgiastic sexuality, for instance, may signify defective sexuality.)

When we look back at the earlier years for data that bear on the sexual hypothesis, we encounter grave confusion at the present time in the meaning of the term sexuality. Melanie Klein, for instance, has employed the term "aggression" to cover many of the manifestations which other psychoanalytically oriented psychologists and psychiatrists call infantile sexuality. (15) Often the "operational indexes" which are used for such terms are ambiguously defined and applied with wavering stability of reference. Whatever words are used to refer to response, environment and predisposition at any cross section of the career line, the significant problem is: to what extent do certain responses which appear in the situation exercise a selective (predis-positional) effect in subsequent situations? It is theoretically possible to tie up descriptions of earlier responses-in-situation with subsequent behavior that is unequivocally political.

We have ample opportunity for examining the composition of groups making use of political symbolism from the period of adolescence onward. (16) The studies that have been made up to the present time give ample confirmation to the significance of dependency and counterdependency demands in relation to leaders. It is not necessary, in the present state of confused though rapidly growing scientific work, to commit ourselves upon the focal significance of the specific indulgences or deprivations that create the low self-estimates on the basis of which these politically significant activities are engaged in.

The fact that we are noncommittal in view of the defective state of present knowledge does not imply indifference. On the contrary: we at once need to enlarge and perfect social institutions that provide us with a continuing survey of the impact of formative environments upon personality.

SOCIAL SELF-OBSERVATORIES OF PERSONALITY FORMATION

We need self-observatories in our society (and throughout the globe) numerous enough and sufficiently well run to provide a continuing audit of the impact of our institutions upon the formation of character and personality. The policy sciences of democracy can then advance more rapidly from their present state of promising though imperfect development to maximum usefulness. What I advocate is an act of institution building for the purpose of carrying on a vital part of the intelligence function essential to the science and policy of democracy.

Mankind is well accustomed to the use of observatories to provide a running account of the physical environment. Beginning with astronomical observatories, we have built institutions that keep us informed about the vagaries of temperature, moisture, wind velocity and barometric pressure; and we use this trend knowledge (analyzed into determining factors) for weather forecasts and even for tentative steps toward control. Observers describe the flora and fauna of land and sea, probe the structural geology of the earth, and lay a finger on the pulse of vulcanism.

Our self-observatories of society are in a less-advanced state. For the most part we confine our systematic reporting of social trends to details that lend themselves to rapid tabulation, such as prices, imports, exports, government receipts and expenditures, births, mortality and morbidity.

We need a never-ending inventory of the character-personality structure (with special reference to the requirements of democracy) of our one-year-olds, our two-year-olds and so on up. These annual cross-sectional patterns can be chosen by proper sampling methods throughout all accessible cultures, all strata in society, and hence during all crisis and intercrisis situations.

Cross-sectional reports can inform us about the constellation of environmental and predispositional factors that are suspected of being important determiners of response. Such reports will enable us to conduct experiments in the future for the sake of determining the usefulness of various methods of changing the environment with a view to aiding the formation of democratic character and personality. When the experiments have been reported, we can adapt the pre-test situations on a larger scale to meet the total needs of democratic society.

By the use of the *World Survey of Personality Formation*

(or of any subsection thereof) we can remove some of the difficulties of articulation that occur among scientific workers themselves, and with decision makers. (17) Wise decision makers must plan ahead to make changes in social routine that can bring about the maximum of desired change throughout society. Scientific work, through lack of a total picture of social structure, often leaves to one side questions of great potential usefulness for policy and of great interest to science.

Today we are uninformed about the speed of development, and the specific nature, of the self structure of infants and children. Data are spotty and inconclusive for the upper, middle and lower power, wealth, respect and other social classes in the United States, to say nothing of other countries. We do not know the precise sequence of indulgent or deprivational secondary symbol formation, with special reference to symbols of authority. There is no mechanism for keeping us up to date on the nature of the values that are supposed to be at the disposal of these images, or the base values by which they can be manipulated.

We are not informed of the tactics actually employed in dealing with the primary circle; or even with the typical structure of the primary circles throughout society. What is the frequency and intensity of the exposure of infants and children of all ages and classes to social stimulation from persons of varying age and other characteristics? Our knowledge of juvenile play groups is sporadic, to say nothing of pre-, mid- and later adolescent groups. The terms used to refer to response, environment and predisposition require more careful "operational definition." Think of the many uses current in theoretical papers and research reports of "domination," "anxiety," "aggression," "aggressiveness," "assertiveness," "infantile sexuality" (for example). Consider the unsatisfactoriness of our indexes of interpersonal relations, especially in view of our crude ways of describing voice and gesture.

The intellectual task of building a satisfactory intelligence survey of personality formation will reduce much current confusion of usage and sectarianism of observational procedure. There are very complex problems of calibration to be solved. Observational procedure A can be very prolonged and specialized (intensive), while procedure B can be relatively brief and simple (extensive). By observing the same (or equivalent) contexts we can, of course, translate results into one another. And within each procedure we can carry calibration through time, which is especially essential since many interpersonal contexts change and the operational indexes of one year change their meaning in relation to the context of last year. (As when a new pattern, like listening to radio broadcasting or watching television or going to nursery school or being allowed a voluntary rather than a strictly dictated feeding schedule, appears.)

NEW INSTRUMENTS OF DEMOCRATIC EDUCATION

A continuing survey of the formation of personality can provide us with knowledge about the most effective use for educational purposes of the new instruments of communication which have been developed in recent years as a result of the "technological revolution." (18) The revolution has provided modern civilization with a tool capable of doing what has never been possible in the past. The new devices have the immediacy of direct experience. Hitherto we have had to rely upon oral presentation or print. It was not possible to reproduce the sights and sounds of concrete human experience. Actually this has been an all but insuperable obstacle to the development of efficient instruction, since the printed page and the spoken word are both inadequate for education in human relations. They are incorrigibly ambiguous. The ambiguity comes from the famous ambiguity of words. The use of the spoken or printed word does not give the teacher sufficient control over the immediate focus of attention of the pupil audience. Hence the word "Chinese" continues to carry private, fantasy-distorted connotations. A printed picture goes further, since it pins down somewhat the autistic processes of the audience. When visual and auditory stimuli are combined, as in the sound film or television, we have far more control over the audience response since the range of ambiguous reference is restricted by "direct" experience. Once anchored in such experiences, a response gains permanence.

By the proper use of sampling it is possible to familiarize the member of an audience with what he would experience were he physically present in representative situations around the globe. We can show the pupil what it is like to be introduced as a stranger to an upper-, middle- or lower-class family anywhere in the world. By dramatic reconstruction, we can carry him through history. Value goals in human relations can be spelled out concretely in terms of the human relations which it is proposed to universalize. Trends can be projected into the future in explicit form.

For the first time we have it within our grasp to attain unprecedented economies in the time spent in effective communication about interpersonal relations. We can take the observing eye of the camera into the laboratory and examine the scientist at work. We can go to the clinic, to rich and poor, far and near.

In a word, by proper sampling we can turn the globe into a village and familiarize every villager with the facts of life.

As a cynical student once remarked to me after a lecture on the potentialities of the film: "Evidently the world can be saved if man can stand the eyestrain." In a sense, this sums it up.

Progressive democratization, therefore, calls for the formation of democratic personality, which is a process of developing character, technique and perspective. As a guide to science and policy, society needs self-observatories capable of exposing the truth about the hidden destructiveness of our cultural institutions, and of reporting on the effect of experimental efforts at reformation. (19)

VIII. LEADERSHIP PRINCIPLES: REDUCE PROVOCATION

PROGRESSIVE democratization calls for the full application of democratic principles to the decision-making process. One major task is to reduce the provocative effect of social institutions. Another task is more affirmative and will be considered after we have given some attention to the negative, precautionary strategy of democratic leadership.

The action principles of democracy depend upon certain skills of thought, as well as management, and after our examination of the positive and negative strategies of democratic management, we will deal with the intellectual skills appropriate to leadership in a free society.

Human destructiveness, as we have previously said, is an outcome of destructive impulses and destructive practices (the latter being destructive because of their provocative effect on impulses). Character is a self-regulating feature of personality, and renders the individual to some extent independent of changes in his environment. But people have different "breaking points," requiring different degrees of external support. Any comprehensive program of democratic statesmanship, therefore, seeks not only to improve the early character-forming practices of society, but to organize all institutions in such a way that provocative crises are kept at a minimum.

ECONOMIC INSTITUTIONS

Some sources of difficulty can be located and dealt with in relatively direct fashion. Scientific study of the dynamics of business cycles can discover the strategic points where controls can be applied for the purpose of reducing the excessive swings of business and of sustaining high levels of productive employment.

John Maynard Keynes performed a notable service for the policy of democratic states by modifying the postulates of economic theory. (1) The traditional conception had been that unemployment was incompatible with a free-market economy, and that joblessness was the result of "frictions." The recurring crises of unemployment, however, suggested the existence of some structural defect in a free-market system. Keynes therefore modified the postulates of the classical theory of a free-market economy, providing a new explanation for the tendency of bad business, once begun, to stay bad rather than to rectify itself automatically. In order to set the system running again, certain governmental activities appear to be essential. Keynesian economics provided a rational basis for government action against unemployment and slack business in place of the traditional program of watchful waiting for the system to rectify itself.

Whatever the merits of the detailed innovations made by Keynes, he emancipated a whole generation of economists from the restraints of a theory that had sterilized fruitful thinking about the structural processes of modern economic society. It became legitimate to build speculative models for the purpose of describing the concrete behavior of economic institutions. (This process is only now beginning to draw the attention of economic theoreticians to the utility of introducing, in systematic fashion, postulates about the noneconomic features of a situation. Soon it will be possible to talk about the behavior of people who *demand* not only goods and services but power and other values; whose *expectations* are composed of expectations not only about goods and services but about power and the other salient values; and whose *identifications* are made explicit, so that they correspond to the existing identifications of living persons with the primary ego, and with the symbols of family, partnership, corporations, nation and so on. When these changes occur, we shall have an economic science that is properly articulated with all the policy sciences of democracy.) (2)

POLITICAL INSTITUTIONS

When we think of reducing the provocativeness of world political institutions, the problem cannot be handled as simply as Mr. Keynes and his colleagues sought to solve the question of how to start the spiral of business up again in a national economy. Mr. Keynes called in the channel of government action. But there is no world government to be called in. The United Nations is not to be confused with an effective instrument of a united world community. The significant problem is to increase the conditions favorable to the progressive transformation of this and similar agencies into effective tools of global action.

THE EXPECTATION OF VIOLENCE

One basic condition of war and tension is the expectation of violence. (3) This is the expectation that, whether you like it or not, it is probable that war will be resorted to as a means of settling acute difficulties. No statesman is serving his country who closes his eyes to the possibility that his best efforts will not bring about and maintain a tolerable peace. He is therefore constrained to carry through a double line of policy, even at the risk of interference between them. One policy is designed to prevent war by perfecting the joint institutions of world community; the other to win a war, should one come. Under these circumstances it is easy for the war mongers to contribute to world tension by stressing the "inevitability" of war, and for the "pacifists" to contribute to war by affirming the "inevitability" of peace, if only you want it hard enough.

THE EXPECTATION OF DISASTER IS NOT ENOUGH

Perhaps it is worth emphasizing the point that the expectation of disaster gives no reliable protection against war. Up to the present time wars could be begun without serious risk that the globe would be destroyed. Even today our physicists cannot guarantee the total destruction of mankind. It is not absolutely certain that chain reactions will reach an uncontrollable pitch of activity and end the story of the earth in a cloud of radioactive dust. Nor is it absolutely sure that biological warfare will exterminate each and every man, woman and child.

For most of us it is sufficiently horrifying that the great centers of population may be annihilated. But horror is not enough to stop war. Whole communities have been annihilated in past warfare (casualties have gone to over half of the population as in parts of seventeenth-century Germany). So long as the expectation of total destruction is not entirely credible, the rulers of a despotic state may prefer the gamble of victorious war to the certainty of losing power at home. Hence a democratically inclined society can be confronted by an antidemocratic regime which prevents the bringing into existence of conditions which reduce the probability of war to zero.

This disastrous result can come about despite good faith on the part of the leaders who bring it to pass. They may at all times act on the basis of the expectation that history speaks through them, and that their form of society is bound to become universal. Further, the expectation may be that universal triumph is bound to come as a result of war which is forced on them by an encircling band of reactionary enemies. (4)

Now you and I may dissent from the conception of an inevitable war. But what if we do? What is there to be done about it? There is no simple method by which power holders in the name of this particular myth can be quickly reached and persuaded of error. Mr. Stalin and the Politburo are not coming to seminars in history, political science and psychology conducted by a "bourgeois" scholar. And there is no record that Mr. Secretary Marshall or his predecessor had much luck as tutors.

PHYSICAL DEFENSE, PSYCHOLOGICAL OFFENSE

Under these circumstances can we learn anything from the policy sciences? The answer is yes. The prescription can be given in a brief formula: Physical Defense, Psychological Offense. (5)

Physical defense means unceasing alertness to the danger of war, and unceasing preparation against this contingency. There must be full and frank disclosure of readiness and capacity to fight. We must be prepared physically to win a war if it suddenly is begun, and we must firmly "contain" the Soviet Union by maintaining our allies from disruption.

Why is this necessary? Because of fundamental laws of behavior as they apply to politics. *There is a strong tendency to repeat whatever succeeds.* If open or secret coercion succeeds, it will, in all probability, be continued. We must make it obvious that coercion does not bring diplomatic or military success.

But this is only part of the available strategy of democratic leadership. The policy of physical firmness must be accompanied by the psychological offensive. The psychological offensive is an appeal to the minds of men, especially of those who are in the intermediate countries. If Russia wins the minds of the young people in countries where there is some freedom of communication, Russian leadership will have every reason to believe that they do in truth represent the wave of the future.

Our psychological task is to win the minds and hence ultimately, and if necessary, the bodies of men, especially in intermediate areas. And it should not be imagined that this is an easy task. For a century a war for the minds of men has been fought in the name of Marxism against feudalism and capitalism. For a century Marxist analysis has been vilified and denied; and yet the plausibility of the socialist diagnosis has borne itself in upon more and more men and women the world over.

This is not solely attributable to zealous propaganda. The Marxist analysis has won its way because it has seemed to be vindicated by so many facts.

For instance, Marxists take credit for having made the forecast that crises of unemployment would get graver. Who is to deny that this is, to say the least, plausible? Marxists take credit for forecasting that private monopolies would become steadily more powerful in capitalistic countries. And who, in view of international cartels and the history of our Antitrust Act, will assert that this is wholly fantastic? Marxists also take credit for the assertion that businessmen, when they feel threatened by proletarian leaders, will support the liquidation of democracy. And who, with Italian fascism,

German nazism and Spanish falangism in mind, will declare that this has nothing to support it?

If our psychological offensive is to succeed, it must be more than "psychological warfare." It must rest upon an interpretation of the past and future that is more universal and compelling than that of our opponents. And this means that the battle for the mind is a battle of expectations. It must be possible for a critical mind to see that, regardless of his personal preferences, certain developments are highly probable.

Later, I shall have some positive suggestions to make about this affirmative program. Let us assume at this point, however, that the psychological offensive is taken. Does this mean war?

Not necessarily. If physical factors are near "50–50," it makes political sense to postpone pushing the fatal "button." If you can be rather sure of keeping your power at home, while the outcome of war is uncertain (except that enormous damage will be suffered), you have a strong incentive to keep "as you were." Under present technological conditions, war between Russia and the United States might not end with *one* Rome but rather with *two* Carthages. (6)

Hence postponement may become a leading characteristic of a highly garrisoned world. Special interests spring up in a perpetual armistice which is characterized by ceremonies of reciprocal vilification. Threat and counterthreat, insult and counterinsult (such as occur in some primitive societies) may develop into major traits of the world community.

Meanwhile internal changes can conceivably bring about a greater sense of security on the part of despotic rulers. As time passes, they can permit some gradual extension of power in the hope of stronger morale in any eventual crisis.

The more democratic states, meanwhile, may acquire more skill in operating an economy at high levels of productive employment.

THE EXPECTATION OF EFFECTIVE RETALIATION

The expectation of violence, therefore, can only be reduced as part of a complex program that ramifies through world society. It is essential to retain the expectation of effective retaliation and to continue a positive campaign for the minds of men.

Concerning the social role of retaliation, let us remind ourselves of the part which expected retaliation plays in some smoothly working societies. When anthropologist Hallowell visited the Salteaux people, he was struck by their politeness and friendliness in dealing with one another and with him. Gradually he learned that this had a potent sanction in the expectation that the other fellow might secretly have more magical power than you had. (7)

Law is socialized retaliation. (8) It is sanctioned by the expectation that severe deprivation will be made against anyone who violates an authoritative rule. In the present world community, we have not yet arrived at the point when we can rely upon collective retaliation in the name of the world community as an adequate sanction. The sanction pattern must therefore be the very difficult and dangerous one of adjusting the mutual values of two great systems of power.

POWER AND SPACE

That the world is polarized around Russia and America is no news today. But it is useful to realize that this is not a capricious development but corresponds to dynamic relations that are rather well understood.

People group themselves in space according to the values they demand, the expectations they entertain about the outcome, and their identifications. It may be useful to put the power-balancing process in perspective by showing how it operates in informal situations, and how even there it can be guided for the purpose of reducing provocation.

An expert hostess has intuitive knowledge of arrangements that reduce the likelihood of disagreeable incidents at dinner parties. Such insights can often be applied to the handling of committees. When seating is undirected, antagonists tend to confront one another, rather than to sit side by side, and followers show a marked tendency to align themselves behind and beside their leaders. In one committee which I observed for several years, a better than chance prediction could be made of the spontaneous seating arrangements at the next session. Those who found themselves in sharp disagreement usually took seats that were more directly opposite or farther from one another than before. (I am glad to report that there was no expectation of violence in this situation, so that problem was not complicated by such considerations as keeping the potential opponent where the light was in his eyes in order to handicap him on the draw, which was a factor in the wild and woolly west.) Generally speaking, the likelihood that persons who confront one another, and are at opposite ends of the available space pattern, will disagree is greater than the probability of disagreement among persons who sit side by side. Shrewd chairmen have sometimes seated possible antagonists beside one another in the hope of avoiding an open break.

These humble though chronic examples of the balancing process are more obvious when large groups are involved, as in the world political arena. When several states of approximately equal strength exist, the balancing process conforms to a recognizable pattern. Owing to the expectation of violence, the two strongest antagonists confront one another, and the lesser powers adjust in relation to them. Although the basic bipolarity of the pattern remains, there may be much shifting of partners. Each power group attempts to penetrate and outflank the other, and the outcome is an organization of space which is often described as "encircled" and "encircling." On the surface of a sphere, such as our earth, all great combinations appear to be "encircling" the other at the boundaries of contact where they confront one another. The situation is most obvious when land powers are involved, as when Germany (before 1914) was aligned with Austria-Hungary against France on the West and Russia on the East. When Britain joined the combination against Germany, control of the sea routes and zones was added to the "encircling" combination.

When two giant powers face each other the pattern of world politics displays the characteristics with which we are today becoming so well acquainted. The world is moving toward relatively permanent segregation in two camps, with little crossing back and forth.

Perhaps it ought to be pointed out that it is not "inevitable" that a two-power pattern of world politics is followed by a universal state. In the past, when all the peoples in significant contact with one another have been under the domination of two great centers, the next step has sometimes been to break up the pattern further and to restore a situation in which several powers emerge. There is no "inevitable" succession of power patterns. Up to the present *all* have been unstable and transitory, including the so-called universal states (monarchies, empires).

Under the conditions of global anarchy which continue

from the dim past into the living present, the task of democratic leadership continues grave and burdensome. The task is how, within a system of mutual provocation, to bring about a situation (by methods short of war) in which retaliation is socialized on a global scale on behalf of the progressive democratization of society. Personalities of unusual maturity and expertness are needed to withstand the anxieties that are so likely to be generated by the chronic uncertainties involved.

THE MENACE OF THE PARANOID IN THE ATOMIC ERA

In coping with our present-day difficulties in the hope of reducing provocativeness, we must not lose sight of the fact that even certainty of annihilation cannot protect us from the paranoid psychotic. If we knew that another war would actually eliminate us, we would not be safe from war. All mankind might be destroyed by a single paranoid in a position of power who could imagine no grander exit than using the globe as a gigantic funeral pyre. And the paranoid need not be the leader of a great state. He can be the head of a small state or even of a small gang.

Even a modicum of security under present-day conditions calls for the discovery, neutralization and eventual prevention of the paranoid. And this calls for the overhauling of our whole inheritance of social institutions for the purpose of disclosing and eliminating the social factors that create these destructive types.

AFFECTION AND RESPECT INSTITUTIONS

Systematic efforts to reduce provocativeness by arranging congenial "teams" of people have only recently been put on a scientific basis in one of the most rapidly expanding fields of the policy sciences. J. L. Moreno and his fellow sociometricians, for instance, have used a number of procedures to elicit from each member of a group information about whom he wants to reside by, work beside or play with. (9) These judgments are charted and the pattern of positive and negative congeniality emerges for the group as a whole and for individuals. Such methods make it possible to explore in detail the relation between various patterns of congeniality and other phenomena, such as leadership.

One interesting point is the connection between congeniality and efficiency. Often congeniality in the work situation comes from respect for (or economic advantage from) the efficiency of a fellow worker. Away from the work place, however, other criteria are applied. Leadership is a complex pattern of congeniality *and* efficiency, and the use of sociometric procedures provides a tool that can be used in our self-observatories to examine the structure of all representative groups. The scattered reports of pioneer students now indicate that the relative significance of specific characteristics is assessed according to the dominant characteristics of the context. If group aims change, so that production skill grows more important (or any other value), we expect that the new situation will activate a different set of predispositions on the part of the participants.

Sociologists of the workplace are recognizing the enormous importance of congeniality for the avoidance of difficulty and for efficiency. One significant result of the factory studies carried on by Elton Mayo and his associates has been a demonstration of the liberating effect of properly constituted work teams. (10) This has long been a standard technique in some educational institutions and in the committee setup of many private associations. In practice, congeniality has always been a factor in determining which workers maneuver for the purpose of staying together at the same bench. But until recent times the full import of this escaped management, furnishing another example of the blindness induced by one-sided emphasis upon the economic and technical features of the work situation.

In politics it is notorious that congeniality is sacrificed for the efficient combination of power elements. Hence the long story of clashing personalities in the cabinet, of tensions in boards and commissions, in committees, and in blocks and coalitions. (Politics does indeed make strange bedfellows.) Efficiency in serving the party often depends on sabotaging the activities of friends. (Hence one of the essential attitudes of the practicing politician is to keep his present resentment at being "deserted" in check, since the deserter may rejoin him on the next issue.)

PERSONNEL ASSESSMENT

One of the practical means by which tensions arising from provocativeness can be reduced is by the selection of leaders from among nondestructive, genuinely democratic characters. It is not within the scope of our present enterprise to enter in detail upon the specific practices by which leaders can be chosen and trained for the proper performance of their functions in the decision-making processes of democracy. At the moment I intend only to underline a single dimension of the selection problem, which is that of developing the assessment of personnel. This has already gone far in appointive jobs. Several businesses are accustomed to promote executives not only on the basis of the general administrative record but according to scientific methods of personality appraisal. The aim is to discern whether factors in the personality structure counterindicate the placing of heavier responsibilities on the person.

To a limited extent selection procedures in army, navy

and civil administration have been directed to the same end. But the procedure is not yet applied to elective office. What is needed is a *National Personnel Assessment Board* set up by citizens of unimpeachable integrity which will select and supervise the work of competent experts in the description of democratic and antidemocratic personality. (11) The Assessment Board can maintain continuing inquiry into the most useful tests and provide direct services or certifications of testers. When this institution has been developed it will slowly gather prestige and acceptance. Sooner or later candidates for elective office will have enough sense of responsibility to submit voluntarily to an investigation by the board, which would say only that the candidate has, or has not, met certain defined minimum standards. Gradually the practice of basic personality disclosure can spread throughout all spheres of life, including not only local, state, national or international government personnel, but political parties, trade unions, trade associations, churches and other voluntary associations.

It is an axiom of democratic polity that rational opinion depends upon access to pertinent facts and interpretations. Surely no facts are more pertinent than those pertaining to the character structure of candidates for leadership. Progressive democratization calls for the development of such new institutions as the Assessment Board for the purpose of modernizing our methods of self-government.

IX.   LEADERSHIP PRINCIPLES:
ACT POSITIVELY

So FAR we have been talking about the avoidance of provocation rather than the affirmative reaching out after democratic results. But there are principles of positive democratic action. *The general strategy is to arouse and maintain expectations of effectively shared values.*

ENLIGHTENMENT (CLARIFICATION)

Consider, from this point of view, the clarification of common goals. The principle of clarification takes into account the undeniable though often neglected fact that men are conscious and can be rational. Human beings resent being left in the dark about the ends of an enterprise in which they are engaged. The act of affirming or admitting a common goal is enough in itself to release human energies to an astounding extent. Many observers have long pointed out that "cadaver obedience" in the sense of the charge of the Light Brigade ("theirs not to reason why") is inefficient. The conquering armies of Allah, of God, of the Emperor, of the Revolution, of Democracy, of the Fuehrer, have all learned to rely upon the use of goal symbols that specify the direction and justification of collective action. To this extent all such movements are democratic, since they pay to everyone the tribute of dealing with him as a "minded organism." (1)

Despite the obvious efficacy of clarification, there are fantastic examples of failures to apply it in practice. A few years ago a study was made of resettlement projects established by the federal government during the depression. (2) Systematic interviewing and participant observation quickly revealed a simple and basic source from which sprang any number of administrative difficulties with which the Farm Security Administration was plagued. Disaffected settlers had no clear conception of the purpose of the projects. They were in the dark about whether the aim was to transform the communities into co-operatives or to leave them in the frame of a non-co-operative economy. Few were clear about whether the federal government would bring about a rapid return to local control, or whether administrative agents of the federal government would continue to exercise a dominant role. In many instances complaints, strikes, sabotage and even wreckage could be traced to these basic confusions.

The central administration in Washington was often under the impression that the directives sent out made everything plain, or at least that the officials on the spot had all the answers and made them available. But communication was taken for granted rather than worked at in detail. Many officials were in the dark about the long-run and middle aims of the central administration. Hence they were in no position to translate policy goals in terms the everyday citizen could understand. There was no systematic check-up on what the citizens thought about the aims and expectations of the enterprise, and consequently but little experimenting with the devices by which more clarity could be brought into the picture. Printed material from national and regional offices was often too technical or sweeping to make contact with local experience.

POWER (CONSULTATION)

Another principle is the sharing of power, or consultation. One of the oldest maxims of government is to pay attention to petitioners. (3) Yet even democratic regimes continually fail to adapt their procedures to the elementary need of giving everybody a voice in what seems to concern him. Giving a voice varies all the way from providing notice and hearing in advance of action (except in dire emergencies) to full plans of representative government. In the problem communities referred to above a genuine grievance was the sense of not being consulted. Changes in housing plans, factory plans or contracts were sudden bolts from the distant blue of "Washington." Advance discussion had not been invited. Settlers felt pushed around on a vast chess board in a game which the individual could not hope to play. This undermined a fundamental expectation upon which democracy depends.

It is entirely consistent with democratic values to vary the degree to which consultation occurs in various situations. In emergencies pre-testing through the ordinary channels of debate produces delays which can be fatal for safety (or other values). In the interest of efficient production the classical business enterpriser has wanted to be free of the obligation to consult, in any formal manner, with anybody else. The traditional argument is that resources are used more efficiently throughout the economy as a whole if business choices are vested in the man who risks his capital. If a worker doesn't like the boss, he can leave and get another job. True, a sacrifice is involved. But the accumulated sacrifices of the workers in moving from job to job are less than the accumulated losses that would result from a more unwieldy policy-making procedure. It is assumed that competitive businessmen and workers are enlightened citizens who have a common interest in policing the market against monopoly, and that the boss and the worker can use agitation, the political party and the ballot to maintain the common framework from whose efficient utilization of resources all benefit.

When competitive freedom is curtailed as jobs in various lines gravitate into a few hands, there is need of more direct sharing in policy. (4) Policy choices which were formerly governed by calculations of economic advantage become transformed, in fact, into power decisions, since they threaten severe deprivation by unilateral action, or are enforcible against dissenters by procedures that entail the application of severe sanctions. The corporation that decides to close down a given plant in the community may inflict severe deprivations upon workers who have invested in homes, paid taxes for municipal services, and developed community life. If there are other plants in the community, the unemployed may be re-employed with a minimum of disorder and at the same level of wages. But if the plant is the only one in the community, the results of the policy are much more severe since it may mean pulling up stakes and going elsewhere. If a unilateral decision depresses the level of employment in the line as a whole, so that the slack is not promptly taken up by competitors or by the opening of comparable opportunities for skills of the same kind, the incidence of the innovation falls heavily upon a few workers. This means that the competitive market has been subtly transformed into a political arena, since a few policy makers exert a disproportionate influence upon the general supply of goods and services.

Where monopolistic-political conditions are found, some means must be invented for representing those affected. Buyers need a means of determining whether the shutting of the plant is part of a monopolistic tactic designed to curtail supply, raise prices and extract monopoly profits. Sellers are similarly concerned with whether the reduced output is part of the tactics of a monopolist to cut costs by forcing down the price of raw and semiprocessed material. Labor has a concern in determining whether the tactic is to beat down labor costs by reducing employment in a given line (and its near substitutes) and thus extracting monopoly advantages. The community is concerned with the fiscal consequences of monopoly, which may narrow the revenue potential (by reducing the total level of economic activity). The community is also concerned with the depreciation of collective services when populations are reduced and with the undermining of democracy which occurs when people are subject to arbitrary exercises of power.

The illustration does not imply that a local community is the unit for organizing full participation in monopolistic-political controls. Actually the scale of organization depends upon the incidence of effects. The control area needs to coincide with the activity area. In some cases local controls will suffice, but the scale may ascend to the regional, national or global level.

The foregoing analysis shows why the expectation on the part of some industrialists is false that the problems of monopolistic-political control can be solved by cultivating consultation at the plant level. Some of the enthusiasm for the "new human relations" has come from owners and managers of monopolistic businesses who hoped to create such a happy situation at the workbench that there will be no motivation for the workers to develop such devices of industrial representation as regional or national or international unions. Industrial sociologists write with enthusiasm of the possibilities of harmonious teams of workers in factories. But they do not have much to say about unions and other structures of control by which workers can protect themselves from monopolistic-political combines. There is too much of the "contented cow" approach to industrial relations, too much emphasis upon getting a level of foremanship that will create stanchions full of contented workers amiably absorbed in local and intimate affairs, having no point of effective contact with the zones of activity which, though beyond their horizon, potently affect their fate.

What is valid in the emphasis upon teams of congenial workers is that progressive democratization is imperiled by frustrated men and women who are driven to support leaders who live by exploiting mass hostilities. When the workers in desperation submit to despotically run labor or party organizations, they are no nearer freedom than before. They have only the choice of exploiters ("capitalist," "union official," "socialist," "communist"). They are caught in a vicious circle that can be broken only to the degree that democratic characters arise who assert themselves so forcefully that the despotizing tendencies of monopoly capitalism and monopoly socialism are checked.

RESPECT (APPRECIATION)

The avoiding of uncongeniality is the negative side of a basic positive principle, which is that of rewarding every deserving person with respect. The principle is "appreciation," parallel to enlightenment and consultation.

The importance of this principle has been brought out in many scientific and managerial situations. (5) The Western Electric Company experiment at the Hawthorne plant, for instance, gave an unanticipated demonstration of its importance. The test team of workers showed a remarkable capacity to raise their level of production, regardless of many changes in the working situation. It should be remembered that these researches were initiated at a time when factory psychology was taken up with "fatigue" and experimenters were reporting on the favorable impact on production of minor shifts in the work situation—painting machines blue, repainting them bright blue, repainting them brighter blue. The output curve of the Hawthorne test group continued to climb *year after year*, despite the fact that among the many experimental changes introduced, some were decidedly unpopular. The obvious inference is that some strong, cumulative factors were affecting the outcome, factors of far greater importance than the piecemeal shifts in the surroundings which had been the stock in trade of applied factory psychologists.

A clue to these hitherto neglected factors is obtained if we note when the production curve ceased to rise and began to drop off. This happened with the great depression. The physical situation of the test team was unaltered, but the *flow* of appreciation from the environment had diminished. During the early years of the research the test room was the center of flattering attention, not only from "big" executives, but from distinguished visitors. The test team began to believe that they were doing something of great importance, not only for themselves, but for all workers in modern industrial society. With these *expectations*, they made *demands* upon themselves to perform at a high level. They *identified* with one another to form a team, and included the nurse and other auxiliaries and supervisors of the experiment. Rising output brought continuing *gratification* from the self thus created; and this gratification was supported by the current appreciation coming from the environment. But when business conditions became bad, executives began to give less attention to the project. The gigantic collapse of business seemed to be the outcome of factors too mysterious, remote and vast to be affected by test-room results. Since expectations about the result became less hopeful, demands upon the self for production grew to be less exacting, and identifications with the "experimental group self" diminished in relation to other parts of the self. Gratifications *of* the self *by* the self, and by people in the environment, became relatively less indulgent and more deprivational.

Two basic points emerge if this interpretation of the results is correct. One: Human beings have great potentialities when they are treated with respect. Two: What can be accomplished in any local situation is limited by the nation-world context. (Hence social strategy must be contextual, selecting significant spots for concurrent action).

RECTITUDE (MORALIZATION)

The principle of rectitude is not to be overlooked. The progressive democratization of society means that democratic activities must be accepted as "right" as well as "expedient." When exposed to an antidemocratic or partially democratic social order, judgments of right and wrong are warped in ways that work against full democracy. The conscience is molded in support of some anti- and some pro-democratic evaluations. Hence the old conscience must be divided against itself and cleansed of its antidemocratic part. White supremacy, for instance, and Aryan superiority are diseased conceptions; so, too, is the notion that the Jew or anybody else is a "chosen" biological category. These are some of the "social paranoias" from which mankind suffers whose progressive therapy and prevention are one of the great objectives of democratic science and practice.

It is perhaps unnecessary to sketch the principles of positive democracy at more length, save to underline the fundamental need of applying the conception of sharing in relation to all values. Shared wealth, in the sense of an ever rising standard of consumption, is evident enough; and so is the sharing of well-being in the sense of a society where safety, comfort and democratic character are accessible to all. The sharing of skill, also, is fundamental since it means providing opportunities to bring talent to the peak of gratifying perfection.

A SPECIAL TECHNIQUE OF ENLIGHTENMENT: INSIGHT

There is one phase of a positive democratic program that deserves more extended discussion in the present setting, and this is the possible dissemination of insight on a vast scale to the adult population. The therapeutic potentialities of insight were first abundantly and scientifically developed by Freud. True, there are precursors in the medical lore of Chinese culture or in the history of Western medicine of the idea that unrecognized drives or wishes can result in illness, and that disorders disappear when order is once more established in the mind. But it was when Freud exploited the potentialities of free association for the treatment and description of disease that the role of insight (or the lack of it) began to take its rightful place.

Quite apart from its utility as a means of therapy, it is only beginning to be understood that free association is a method of using the mind on a par with reflective thinking, and that, like any true method, it can be deliberately cultivated. The principal advantage of free association (or free fantasy thinking) is that it brings into the full focus of waking awareness significant data that are inaccessible to the disciplined routines of strictly guided thinking. The free-association method can acquaint the thinker with aspects of himself that have an important bearing on his problems, especially when they directly concern his relations to people. I refer, of course, to the type of self-knowledge that was exemplified in the *Psychopathology of Everyday Life* and that becomes part of the skill of successfully analyzed persons.

There is nothing new in the Socratic maxim "Know Thyself." But something new was added when a procedure was developed for making it possible to put this admonition into daily practice. So much of our civilization is full of argument and debate that one major intellectual skill in dealing with people is dialectic. The person who can't put up a plausible reason on behalf of a demand is a very handicapped member of the community. The man, woman or child who can add an "ought" to a simple "want" is more likely to get by than the one who isn't quick with the "oughts."

The Greeks settled many public affairs by argument and the mode of talking and thinking appropriate to this sort of activity was developed into the principles of dialectic. (6) Today we are dimly aware that too much emphasis has been given to dialectic, and that other ways of talking and thinking are needed to supplement it. The spread of scientific interest has led to the use of postulational constructs with an eye to their usefulness in observing nature. (7) As man learns to look at himself as part of the world of events, these ways of using the mind are progressively applied to the whole context of interpersonal relations. And it begins to appear that one of the necessary ways to obtain the data about the self called for by the postulational systems is to forget about postulates, for the time being, and allow the mind to flow freely and to disclose the impulses that are pressing toward expression. Instead of springing into postulational or dialectical activity, many people have learned to pause for self-disclosure.

What is disclosed is often incompatible with the conscious ends of the person, and must be rejected. By bringing the impulse into waking awareness, it can be deprived of much of its indirect strength in defeating the ends of a person (who, for instance, is consciously devoted to democratic goal values). Persistent self-examination can go a very considerable distance in enlarging the part of the personality whose resources are made available for the ends sought.

There was a time when insight therapists and researchers were disposed to pooh-pooh the idea that very much could be accomplished through insight outside the prolonged psychoanalytic interview situation. But in recent years there are abundant signs that this sectarian viewpoint is much relaxed. Indeed, we live in a period in which the terrain between the psychoanalyst and the spot interpreter of behavior is being rapidly filled in. Every observational procedure from the most *intensive* to the most *extensive* is being occupied, and every form of insight therapy is being tried out. Karen Horney devotes a book to self-analysis. (8) Alexander, French and associates report on abbreviated methods of fostering insight. (9) Psychiatrists write of their experience at the front where they were able by brief, energetic explanations to prevent a crackup. (10)

All this raises in more acute form than ever the possibilities of reducing destructive tendencies throughout society by a combined therapeutic operation that employs many patterns of interpersonal intervention.

There is, of course, the *one-to-one* procedure of the *prolonged* interview. Ten thousand interviewers putting in ten hours a day, six days a week, represent 600,000 hours per week or 31,200,000 hours a year. Colossal as this sounds, it would take care of only 200,000 individuals a year if each one averaged six months.

There is also the *one-to-one* procedure with *brief* contact. And this is the trend of recent experimentation in military and civilian circles. Trained personnel can (in principle) be made available for every significant human situation, and ways worked out of winning not only introduction but acceptance.

And there are the *one-to-few* patterns with either brief or prolonged *expert* supervision, such as are being tried out most actively in the experiments in group therapy. (11)

In addition, we must recognize the growing importance of the one-to-few patterns which have no direct supervision by experts but which model their methods on what may be called the "new common sense," which means the enhanced level of lay critique which modern scientific advance has made possible. A striking instance is the treatment of alcoholism by methods of group therapy in which a group of laymen take over the burden of providing an environment in which a specific pattern of conduct is taken as the problem. (12) The same principle can be extended to many patterns of social conduct, and with every conceivable degree of lay-expert co-operation.

We must not overlook the *one-to-many* pattern (or the few-to-many pattern), since many of the changes now going forward in our civilization stem from the degrees of enlightenment purveyed through the channels of mass communication. There are doubtless debits as well as credits in the account, but from the standpoint of clarity of human understanding the complications that come from partial insight are to be preferred to the complications of innocence. ("Innocence" is the prelude to the first steps toward insight.)

The mass media of communication are already full of many forms of psychological and social explanation of human response. (13) Too many of these items are open to criticism for the degree to which they rely upon purveying the results rather than the procedure of understanding. There are not enough stories of the route, often tortuous and frequently interesting, by which insight dawns.

This is a place where psychiatric observations can be usefully harnessed to the task of general enlightenment. Every professional and occupational group has its own perspective and best comprehends what is addressed to it when its own language is used. Materials that show how administrators have gained insight, or how judges have caught on to themselves, are certain to make a heavier impact on colleagues than on the public at large. And if these materials are presented in a way that conveys some inkling of how insight was obtained (when it occurred), so much the better. (14)

By the preparation of film and other materials, the process of observation can be exemplified with enough concreteness to prod the audience-member into more and clearer self-knowledge. (15)

We must not overlook the possible use of narco- and hypnoanalytic aids to the general reduction of tension in the community. (16)

And there is always the possibility of furthering the slow and intricate task of mass insight by the skillful use of mass media for the purposes of indirect teaching. Donald Duck is a stock example. This cartoon image stands for the one who loses self-control; and he enables a person to laugh at his own foibles, as well as to be reminded of them when he approaches the quacking point. Mass therapy of destructive prejudices may be facilitated by this method.

Our social observatories can keep us informed of the effectiveness of available means of reducing the level of destructive anxiety in adults as well as in children.

LEADERSHIP THINKING

The foregoing analysis of insight forms a convenient transition from the strategies of democratic management to the intellectual skills adapted to the tasks of leadership in a free society. The management strategies are both negative and positive, taken up in the first instance with reducing the provocativeness of social institutions, and in the latter with maintaining expectations of effectively shared values. The training of democratic leaders must include the action strategies. But that is not enough, since the ends and timing of management need to be subordinated to a comprehensive intellectual conception. In the broadest sense, the essential skills of the mind are twofold, including observation and thinking. The use of free association is, in this perspective, a method of self-observation, whose fruits contribute pertinent data for reflection.

Several skills of thought are desirable equipment for the citizen-leader of a democratic society. (17) I speak of them here as goal thinking, derivational thinking, trend thinking, scientific thinking and projective thinking; taken together they constitute the configurative method. (18)

GOAL THINKING

Among the basic skills of thought is goal thinking, the practice of clarifying the aims of action, hence of democratic policy. We cannot afford to have leaders who are in a fog about the meaning of democracy. We have already taken care to say that this is more than word matching, in which a formula like the dignity of man is repeated as a bit of ritual, after the fashion in which Sun Yat-sen's Three Principles are intoned at gatherings of Kuomintang officials. Words about goal values are necessarily words of somewhat ambiguous reference, and we cannot wisely try to settle their meaning by simple definition. There are always open issues that call for further observations designed to clarify for rational judgment the probable effects of this or that environing and predisposing factor in the impact on response. Our democratic leaders must be accustomed to operate in this world of partial clarity and to think always in terms of what is true by definition and what is true by observation; and to accustom themselves to a harmonious interplay between conceptual definition, operational definition and data from social self-observatories. (19)

DERIVATIONAL THINKING

Besides goal thinking there is derivational thinking. (20) This is the technique, for instance, of justifying the dignity of man by invoking statements of higher abstractness, such as God's will or the metaphysical principle of light or darkness. Let me confess for myself that I have little interest in derivational thinking, which consists in substituting one set of self-selected ambiguities for another, and demonstrating that the least ambiguous can be logically derived from the most ambiguous. But I know that mankind has a heavy burden of religious and philosophical symbols, and that many groups and persons are uncomfortable and ineffective if they cannot invoke them to legitimize the goal of human dignity. And I speak for those who wish to work with anyone who shares the objective, regardless of whether he derives it from religion or philosophy.

TREND THINKING

Besides goal thinking and derivational thinking, there is trend thinking. This might be called historical or chronological thinking, since what is meant is that one undertakes to locate one's self in the stream of events, and to know the degree to which goal values are realized. (21)

SCIENTIFIC THINKING

Factor thinking (scientific thinking) proceeds by formulating generalizations, confirmable by observation, of the determinative relationship among goal variables and the variables that condition them. Scientific thinking calls for expertness in forming postulational systems, as well as in relating such systems to procedures of observation by the choice of operational definitions and by the development of adequate social self-observatories.

PROJECTIVE (DEVELOPMENTAL) THINKING

Another pattern is projective thinking, which implies a picture of the future, a picture of the alternatives by which goals are likely to be affected by what we, or anyone else, will probably do. Hence projective thinking includes the evaluation of newly *invented* ways of moving toward the goal, and embraces the products of creative imagination about the ways and means of policy.

CONFIGURATIVE THINKING

Democratic leaders need to think configuratively and to apply all the skills just outlined. For maximum rationality it is necessary to use each tool, with no excessive reliance upon one. Each tool is part of the total process by which the mind can seek and perhaps find correct orientation in the entire manifold of events that are important for progressive democratization. Some events are in the future: they are goals and projections. Some are in the past and are events of which we can have knowledge, since they can rest at any given moment upon data of observation. (22)

In some ways the thinking in the United States about human relations has been unnecessarily one-sided in the amount of emphasis put upon derivation (justification) and upon science. This has meant a relative de-emphasis upon the *clarifying* of goals, the *projection* of future developments, including especially the *invention* of future lines of policy. The significance of this one-sidedness is seen in the belated development of the policy sciences to a point where knowledge is mustered for clear-cut objectives, and is fully related to the most likely contingencies to appear in the unfolding processes of history.

In some ways the most crippling lack has been of comprehensive projections into the future. This mode of thinking is indispensable for responsible action, which invariably consists in selecting programs in the light of expectations about future contingencies. No one plans a military campaign, a party program or a business enterprise without modifying his conceptions of policy in the light of estimates of what will happen under various circumstances. For instance: Will the opposition press take the offensive early in a campaign and stir up latently hostile elements in the electorate? Can a countercampaign succeed if the debate is precipitated as early as possible? Are there demands which, if incorporated in the program, will split the opposition? Are there candidates and policies available to the rival group

that will succeed in splitting off the support with which one
begins the campaign? Such questions are representative of
the queries which every experienced politician faces when
choices are before him.

X.   CAPITALISM, SOCIALISM AND
OUR HISTORICAL PERIOD

THIS concluding chapter will provide an exemplification
of what is meant by projective (or developmental) thinking
about the dominant political possibilities of our epoch. In
offering this provisional picture of things to come, several
purposes may be served. Undoubtedly the panorama will
clarify what is meant by one of the skills of thought which
have been recommended as a desirable part of the equipment of democratic leaders (and citizens). Furthermore, the
specific "construct" herein described may provide an incentive for the use of other intellectual skills. Goal thinking,
for example, may be restimulated, since if his value-objec-
tives touching upon human dignity have been defined too
narrowly in the past, the reader may reopen the question.
(Has he confused *values* with a specific set of economic, political and social *institutions* to which his parochial experience has given him uncritical attachment?) In addition
to goal thinking, the reader may re-examine his assumptions about trends, criticizing, for instance, his expectations
about the triumph of "socialism" or "capitalism," in so far
as they are founded upon knowledge of changes occurring
in recent history. Going further, the reader may make an
inventory of his scientific knowledge, especially the "laws"
of "material" or "ideological" development. And more:

recognizing the peril to his democratic values in the impending future, the reader may think inventively about how to use his knowledge (of power, for instance) to protect or advance his threatened goals. For constructs about the future are only probable, not "inevitable"; and successful use of the mind can be part of the historical process itself, interacting with other parts of the process to obviate occurrences which would otherwise take place. Such intellectual operations may point the way toward positive or negative strategies of democratic management.

DEVELOPMENTAL CONSTRUCTS

Note that expectations about the future are not scientific propositions, although they are hypotheses about the shape of things to come. Let us call them *developmental constructs* in order to distinguish them from scientific hypotheses, laws and principles. A sample developmental construct is the statement from socialist-communist doctrine that "the trend of historical development in our era is from capitalism to socialism." The term "capitalism" is taken to refer to a pattern of institutions approximated in various countries at a given period in the past. The term "socialism" refers to a pattern of social institutions alleged to receive global distribution at a future period. A statement of this kind can at any given moment be taken as the point of departure for gathering and appraising data about trends and conditions on a global scale.

Contrast this with an intellectual operation that takes a scientific proposition as the starting point. The statement may be that the degree of socialization of property depends upon the technological interdependence of the processes of production. Hence as the means of production become more interdependent, the concentration of control will increase.

In order to confirm (or refute) such a proposition, data can be sought from the comparative analysis of societies in the past, from the intercorrelation of factors in recent trends, or in experimental situations.

For our purposes it is important to take note of the fact that intellectual operations beginning with a scientific proposition differ from operations whose point of departure is a developmental construct. The point is not whether these taking-off places are logically consistent or inconsistent. (It can be demonstrated that developmental constructs can be readily derived from certain scientific postulates, and conversely, that scientific postulates can be derived from developmental constructs.) To use a pat and often misleading expression, the difference is "psychological, not logical." This means that effective ways of using the mind are vastly stimulated by reliance upon one or another mode of approaching a problem.

A truly configurative method is a tool of thought because it can be deliberately used for the purpose of gaining orientation in the manifold of events in which the thinker functions. Progressive democratization as a future goal calls for trend, factor and projective thinking; and the thinker can rely first upon one line of attack upon his problem, then another. By moving back and forth from one "lead in" to the next, he can increase the likelihood of arriving at policies that facilitate democracy.

THE ALLEGED SEQUENCE FROM CAPITALISM TO SOCIALISM

The configurative mode of approach has been advocated and approximated in varying degrees by many men. Marx and Engels were setting up a developmental construct when they postulated the passage of history from capitalism to socialism. They rejected as "mechanistic" the forms of thinking that had no place for other than what we call scientific propositions. They made a mistake when they confused their developmental construct with a scientific law, imputing to it the "inevitability" of a proposition that summarizes data of observation. An assertion about the "inevitability" of future events is propaganda and ought not to be confused with scientific or developmental statements. The future cannot be known in advance; it can be estimated in terms of probability.

The capitalism-to-socialism sequence was set forth in this way: The technical revolution in the tools of production by modern science was alleged to bring about profound changes in the division of labor and hence in the class structure of society. The principal effect was said to be the concentration of private ownership and control in the hands of a few; and this, in turn, initiated a countermovement, led by a dictatorial few who by substituting a generalized pattern of ownership and control through socialization not only abolished by a revolutionary leap the concentration of wealth but in this way laid the economic foundation for democratization after a brief dictatorial transition.

FROM CASTE SOCIETY TO FREE SOCIETY

The Marxist construct was one of the many forms of assertion about the future that were invented in nineteenth-century Europe, and shared many of the same features. Progress was postulated in the form of impending transition into a free society from caste societies. (1) A society is properly classified as a caste society when the position of each person in the social structure depends upon the position of the family into which he is born. The feudal-monarchical society was, in the minds of political thinkers, the prototype of the hereditary transmission of status and the concentration in a few families of overwhelming command over power, wealth, respect and other values. Modern capitalism was said by Marx to have been anticaste at first, since the private owners of the means of production successfully widened the access to wealth by displacing the feudal-monarchical elite based on land. At a later stage, it was alleged, capitalism began the formation of a small ruling caste of its own from whose domination the new industrial proletariat would free themselves through world revolutionary cataclysm.

Capitalism developed its own conception of history, although not in the elegant form contrived by Marx and Engels. Partly in reply to socialist criticism and partly on the basis of known historical facts, the apologists of capitalism agreed with the socialists about the "inevitability" of progress, which they identified with the spread over the globe of the free market and free government.

Socialists and capitalists were therefore in accord in condemning the caste society of the feudal-monarchical era and in pronouncing a sentence of inevitable death upon it. They jointly held out the optimistic expectation that the free society was just around the corner. The socialists expected the occupants of the leading car in the procession to take a serious spill as history went around the corner. Free-enterprise democrats expected to make a smooth turn.

HAS HISTORICAL DEVELOPMENT REVERSED DIRECTION?

Today there is grave reason for believing that both interpretations are in error and in fact contribute in varying degrees to defeating their common purpose and confounding their own predictions. Socialism and capitalism are in the same boat, and the boat is sinking. It may not be saved in time.

THE ERRORS OF "FREEDOM BY WORLD REVOLUTION"

Dealing first with the Marxist construct: Marx left at least two major possibilities out of account, and both possibilities are the ones most likely to contradict the speculative model of the future that was projected by the Marx-Engels school of socialism. Marx-Engels followed the effects of the new technology to the point of emphasizing its initial impact on the old feudal society, and forecast its future effect on the concentration of production in a few hands. But the possibility was overlooked that the terrific tempo of technoscientific expansion would *put the controlling few on opposite sides of frontiers* and unleash a war in which the globe itself would vanish or both warring power constellations would suffer unprecedented losses (two Carthages; not one Rome).

The second neglected major possibility is that the leaders of the territorially distinct power systems will postpone war indefinitely, prolonging crisis in order to consolidate their power in new caste societies, in this way transforming the globe into a world of garrison (or police) states dominated by small hereditary castes recruited from specialists on the administration of modern technoscientific instruments of violence. In this way the tendency toward democratization which was stimulated during the early stages of the application of modern science to technology would be reversed, blocking the historical trend of recent times in the direction of free societies and substituting a trend toward caste societies run by military-police families.

If this outcome is probable, and recent trend and factor knowledge is in harmony with it, the doctrines of revolutionary socialism are not only in error. By a tragic paradox not unusual in history, they are themselves factors in defeating their aims and prophecies. All wings of revolutionary Marxism unite in imagining a future in which progressive democratization is the automatic gift of world revolution. The Stalinist users of the vocabulary of revolutionary social- ism say that the world revolution will become universal toward the end of the world war in which monopoly capital- ists try to put down the Soviet Union by force. The Trotsky- ists expect world revolution to come at the end of a possible series of revolutions, one of which might well mark the liquidation of the Stalinist despotism which they accuse of betraying the world proletariat and world socialism. (2)

And both, if the present construct is correct, are in error. No movement, including the one toward democratization, is "inevitable." And if world currents continue at their pres- ent tempo, world democratization is drastically improbable. The free society becomes possible only on the basis of certain conditions, and one of these conditions is the deliberate and successful effort of genuine democrats to expose the dubious and dangerous expectation of democracy through mass revolution.

THE ERRORS OF DILATORY CAPITALISM

The writers and men of action who hammered out the ideology of the modern business state lulled themselves into a false sense of security which, when rudely interrupted by recent developments, led to an equally erroneous interpreta- tion of their insecurity.

The false sense of security came from the seeming triumph of modern business in carrying the world toward one big market where men would trade peacefully and progress ma- terially and culturally.

Like the socialists, the free enterprisers forgot about the relative importance of war, revolution and the expectation of violence. Wars and violence were dismissed as regrettable "frictions" that would rub away in a sea of universal plenty. The One Big Market was equivalent to One Big Socialist Brotherhood: both were, by definition, characterized by democracy, abundance, morality, respect. These were interchangeable myths of the free society. In one, the benefits came from the Perfect Market. In the other, from Perfect Government. (3)

Both myths were, by definition, perfect. And each, when confronted by disagreeable facts, led their interpreters to attribute the facts to "friction" or to unrecognized intrusions of the other system (which was by definition the quintessence of imperfection).

Capitalism and capitalists were dilatory about putting their myth into practice. They did not succeed in stabilizing high levels of productive employment in any large territory. Instead, business states opened up more and more new territory to trade and investment, postponing the evil day when something must be done about the failure of the system to live up to the myth of full and efficient use of resources. By expanding unstable economies over larger areas, they made possible bigger booms and busts. Nevertheless, it continued to be assumed, without demonstration, that the economy that could not stabilize itself in North America or in Western Europe would stabilize as soon as it added Asia, Africa and the rest of the globe.

And how? This question was typically evaded by policy makers and their advisers. It was "theoretical." The issue was postponed. One result was that the measures essential to check the silent transformation of genuinely competitive markets (where such existed) into monopoly-political arenas were not taken. Hence the economy that was supposed to be stabilized was shot through with so many noncompetitive and political features that the myth was an example of dubious if not false labeling.

Dilatory capitalism had become something else (or remained the same, if you take the view of some historians that the degree of concentration has been remarkably constant). Capitalism was being transformed into a political organization which concealed its nature by speaking the language of "business," "competition," "free enterprise" and the like. In this political organization an intense struggle for power was, and is still, being carried on between various rival groups.

One group is the *monopoly-politicians*. They are the owners and managers of private monopolies. Falsely calling themselves "businessmen" (rather than politicians), they invoke the symbol "business" to line up what is left of genuinely competitive business behind them in an effort to prevent the application of democratic methods of control to their arena of arbitrary power.

Another group is the *party politicians* who serve themselves by serving every interest, and who, as the conflict over monopoly intensifies, themselves gain power. In some cases, as in Germany and Italy, the party politicians, receiving money from many sources (and especially from monopoly politicians), take over the key spots in society. In the process they not only liquidate the residual fragments of private business but subdue the monopoly politicians (or, speaking more precisely, combines of certain party leaders—whose skill is agitation and party administration—are made with certain monopoly leaders; these combines squeeze out their rivals). (4)

Another group is the *government officials*. During the phase of active transition from democratic and competitive conditions, the government officials play second fiddle to the party politicians and the monopolists in the control of society.

Another major element in the power struggle is the *officers* and *policemen* (and especially the political police). They are the ones who benefit most from sustained crisis.

It may be noted in passing that the groups referred to are recruited from somewhat distinctive skills, which in turn are congenial to various character types. The monopoly politician adds to the businessman's basic skill in bargaining, skill in negotiation, which is the making of agreements sanctioned by more values than money. The party politician is a *symbol specialist* or a party *administrative expert*. The official also relies chiefly on skill in administration. Policemen and soldiers are *specialists on violence,* which, under modern conditions, is typically combined with great administrative responsibility.

Tormented by their insecurities, businessmen and monopoly-politicians, when confronted by rival politicians who invoke a socialist vocabulary, are sorely tempted to embark on a war to "restore freedom" by opening up areas to the "world market" that have been excluded from it by political means. This alternative drives the genuinely competitive businessman and the civilian monopolist into the arms of the military and the police, whether in preparation for war, or in the attempt to administer "conquered" territory. Under modern conditions the active phase of fighting must be followed by prolonged military and police measures in order to protect a new regime against subversion. The expectation of violence is not to be abolished by war, but rather it is transformed into a pervasive fear of assassination, sabotage and the renewal of war from secret laboratories. The only ones to benefit (in the sense of occupying favorable places in the social structure) from war are the warriors and policemen as a class.

Dilatory capitalism, therefore, finds itself partly transformed into a political order, uncertain what to do next. One prognosis, at least, is highly probable: *War will not restore business but consolidate the military and the police in a garrison-caste state.* (5)

WHAT MAKES SENSE?

Under what conditions is it rational to expect the trend toward freedom to be resumed? One condition is clarification in the thinking not only of socialists but of businessmen as well.

The issue of our historical period is not socialism *or* capitalism but socialism *and* capitalism together *against* the annihilation of mankind, or serfdom in a world of garrison-prison states: the issue is the progressive democratization of the world community. We do not necessarily have socialism when the tools of production are concentrated in a few hands. It is certainly not capitalism when the tools of production are concentrated in a few hands. Both are blocked when the generals or the police or the monopoly politicians or any despotic concentration of power occurs.

In the name of socialism, socialism can fail. In the name of free enterprise, business can be betrayed. In fact, the crisis of today is bigger than the frame of economic life. The degrees of freedom inside a world of garrison-police states are *less* than required by socialist or capitalist doctrine to allow either economic system to continue.

The conception that war is a prelude to inauguration of a free socialist society is no longer tenable. Neither is the conception that war can restore business freedom. The fact is that more and more people are becoming aware of the double threat to life and liberty which is inseparable from the use of modern science and technology for war and chronic preparation for war. These "material" facts are "impressing" themselves on millions of apprehensive men and women everywhere. This is part of the enlightenment process in society, a process that can be accelerated as part of a psychological offensive designed to free mankind of suicidal illusions about the "inevitability" of freedom by catastrophe. By enlightenment initiatives can be released (especially by way of the intermediate countries) for the *escape to freedom* by the continuing postponement and ultimate prevention of war.

THE CONTEXTUAL PRINCIPLE

Besides having a hand in the task of enlightening mankind about the dangers connected with ideologies of inevitability, we can disseminate an affirmative point of view toward the "possible." The basic viewpoint has already been described in connection with the negative and positive strategies of democratic management. Putting the two together, and combining them with the configurative method of thinking, we speak of the contextual principle. The contextual principle provides us with a rational basis for saying that the mastery of the opportunities of the technoscientific age can come not by dogmatic reliance on a single scheme of organizing life but from the flexible development of contexts that promote the sharing of all values. Every situation, no matter how comprehensive or how restricted, affords some opportunity to apply this principle. It can become a guiding conception for private and public policy of those who accept the value goals of democracy.

From the policy sciences and especially from psychology,

psychiatry and sociosomatic medicine, the contextual principle is receiving new confirmation. The principle can be stated in many ways. One of the simplest: *The meaning of any detail depends upon its relation to the whole context of which it is a part.* Hence any cultural detail, such as a statement of doctrine or a technical operation, has no unalterable meaning for society; this depends upon the context of which it is a part.

Gestalt psychologists have demonstrated the principle most convincingly. (6) In the field of perception psychoanalysis has abundantly exemplified it in the data obtained by free association. Physiologists like Walter B. Cannon have underlined the importance of searching for an entire equilibrium of interacting variables when studying organic processes, rather than correlating between discrete items. (7) Elton Mayo and his coworkers deliberately sought to think contextually about factory sociology. An outstanding anthropologist like Bronislav Malinowski vivified a whole field of social study by his insistence upon putting each detail in a functional context that included the culture as a whole. (8) Psychiatric and psychosomatic (sociosomatic) medicine are rich with exemplifications of this principle.

Up to the present we have made only sporadic applications of the contextual viewpoint when social institutions are involved. We continue to allow statements to pass unchallenged to the effect that this or that doctrine has specific effects, regardless of the context. Yet common experience reveals that even the person who sincerely believes in the general principle of human dignity can have antidemocratic effects. He may, for instance, find it difficult to apply in practice to members of ethnic groups. He may not have noticed that he bullies his wife and spoils his daughter; or that he condones a monopolistic practice. And the same inconsistencies and contradictions are commonplace. True believers, in the sense of subjective sincerity, in Christianity, Judaism, and any other system of religious doctrine can fight on opposite sides in war and revolution.

Conceptions like "ownership of property" are of the utmost ambiguity, covering degrees of effective control that range from one extreme to another. (9) The doctrines of property law are in perpetual flux, since they are being invoked in widely different situations to obtain widely scattered results. To say that something is owned or leased tells you nothing whatever about the factual context until you have conducted exhaustive factual inquiries. To say that something is privately or governmentally owned also tells you nothing about the degree of effective control over resources. Field investigation can show that more effective control is exercised by those who lease from the government than from certain private owners, and vice versa.

When you think contextually, it becomes clear that we are accustomed to use words like "socialism," "capitalism," "private property," "government property," "competition," "monopoly" and such with no stable designative meaning. In the mouth of a leader of public opinion and sentiment, these are emotive symbols of ambiguous reference. Specialists add to the confusion when they neglect to warn the audience that the technical definition of a small corps of experts has little if any relation to what the layman thinks the expert is talking about. (10) The layman gives conventional meaning to words like "government," "politician," "market," "businessman." But the expert has a rigorous system of postulates which can be at variance with the layman's ideas. In the present book, for example, we have carefully distinguished between the conventional and functional definition of "government," showing how, from a functional standpoint, government (power) might be exercised by business corporations or trade unions. This has enabled us to make a more rigorous separation than usual between a "businessman" (in the sense of classical economics) and the "monopolist-politicians," with whom businessmen are so often confused. Similarly it is important to distinguish between "socialism" and forms of "non-socialist collective ownership" in which effective control actually rests with a self-perpetuating bureaucracy which manages production for its own purposes, rather than in order to elevate the living standard of the masses. In the same way, "capitalism" needs to be thought of separately from "non-capitalist private ownership," since the latter case can apply to a plantation run like a prison farm.

When we use the contextual principle to remove the ideological blinders from our eyes, it becomes obvious that "pure" socialism or capitalism, like "pure" democracy or "despotism" have seldom been approximated. Furthermore, within any given institutional context, modifications toward greater or less shaping and sharing of democratic values are possible. Within a highly centralized, concentrated, and regimented setup, for instance, it may favor the sharing of power, respect, and enlightenment to work toward more decentralization, deconcentration and deregimentation. The same purposes may be served in some situations, on the contrary, by moving toward more authority and control at the center.

More generally, the role of practically any detail of personality and culture *can* have either a destructive or nondestructive significance, depending upon the context of which it is a part. Hence the analytic-managerial problem is to weaken or sustain contexts, rather than isolated items of dogma, slogan, key symbol, or technique.

The use of the contextual principle entails, and fortifies, detachment from exaggerated stress upon this or that doctrine or operation. The aim alone is constant: we are concerned with the progressive democratization of mankind. The task is to search for every conceivable means in every available situation.

Looking back over the course we have come in this book, it is possible to summarize by saying that the sciences of democracy have already contributed greatly to the understanding of where mankind stands in the historical process. Especially, we have enough knowledge of how to obtain knowledge to see the necessity of inventing social self-observatories and other institutions capable of providing a rational basis for the expansion of democratic science and policy.

The accentuation of power, we have suggested, is compensation against estimates of the self as weak, contemptible, immoral, unloved. Personalities fit to participate in the democratization of society must love themselves enough to love all. Progressive democratization depends upon finding the ways of dealing with children which do, in fact, aid in the formation of democratic character, transmit democratic perspectives and foster the acquisition of democratic skills. The principles of democratic action need to be supplemented by adequate methods of thought.

Today mankind has a common, though dimly seen, task which is the discovery of ways and means of realizing human dignity. There is a world community which is sufficiently well-developed to endanger itself and not sufficiently developed to release the full value-shaping and sharing potentialities of a democratic commonwealth.

Standing in the path of further progress is the socialist-capitalist expectation of benefit from war and revolution. The contextual principle puts us on guard against taking words like "socialism" or "capitalism" too seriously. Actually it makes more sense to think of modern society as "sociocapitalist," though threatened by the regimentation of a garrison-police state. Only antisocialist and antibusiness elements in society stand to gain from chronic crises. They are the potential rulers of a world concentration camp, the specialists on the administration of military and police violence, who may succeed in reversing the trend of history from the free society to the restoration of a caste society.

There is nothing "inevitable" about the future. But there are possibilities of varying degrees of probability. And our task as scientists of democracy is to affect policy while yet there is time. We *can* aid the progressive transformation of human society into a free man's commonwealth.

NOTES
AND
INDEX

NOTES

CHAPTER I

1. Samuel Butler, *Miscellaneous Thoughts.*
2. Henry Adams, *The Education of Henry Adams,* chs. 10, 16.
3. Shaw Desmond, *World-Birth,* part I.
4. Thomas Paine, *Common Sense.*
5. William Godwin, *An Enquiry Concerning Political Justice.*
6. Friedrich Engels, *Schriften aus der Frühzeit* (1842–44). See also Hans J. Morgenthau, *Scientific Man vs. Power Politics.*
7. Lynn Thorndike, *A History of Magic and Experimental Science during the First Thirteen Centuries of Our Era,* vol. I, ch. 14.
8. The humbler figures occasionally get a good word, as when L. D. White and T. V. Smith say (in *Politics and Public Service*) that "the democratical politician alone stands between us and dictatorship. . . . He . . . works out compromises on the frontiers of violence so as to extend the boundaries of tolerance."
9. See E. C. Tolman, *Purposive Behavior in Animals and Men,* and Clark L. Hull, *Principles of Behavior.*
10. Time-distribution data are in J. S. Henderson and H. J. Laski, "A Note on Parliamentary Time and the Problem of Devolution," *Economica,* vol. 5 (1925), pp. 89–93.
11. It is one merit of Chester I. Barnard (*The Functions of the Executive*) to have emphasized the continuity of response involved in leadership. See also P. Pigors, *Leadership or Domination;* Denys O. W. Harding, *The Impulse to Dominate;* Ordway Tead, *The Art of Leadership.*

12. The treatment of "power" follows that of H. D. Lasswell and Abraham Kaplan, which is briefly summarized in the appendix of this book.

13. Consult C. E. Merriam, *Systematic Politics;* R. M. MacIver, *The Web of Government;* Gaetano Mosca, *The Ruling Class;* Roberto Michels, *Political Parties;* Vilfredo Pareto, *The Mind and Society;* Ernest Barker, *Reflections on Government;* G. E. G. Catlin, *The Science and Method of Politics;* Max Weber, "Wirtschaft und Gesellschaft," *Grundriss der Sozialökonomik,* III Abteilung.

14. See Jacob Viner, "Political Aspects of International Finance," *Journal of Business,* vol. I (1928), pp. 141–73, 324–63; Robert A. Brady, *Business as a System of Power;* David Lynch, *The Concentration of Economic Power;* Robert A. Gordon, *Business Leadership in the Large Corporation;* Beardsley Ruml, *Tomorrow's Business;* John R. Commons, *Legal Foundations of Capitalism* and *Institutional Economics.*

15. Power is not necessarily *law,* if the term law is deliberately reserved for authorized sanctions administered in the name of the whole community by the entire community (or a specialized representative) in a regular manner. And we know that there are communities in which there is no court, police or method by which everyone acts concurrently to name and inflict deprivations upon an offender. Parts of the community may act, but they do so in the name of a smaller unit of the whole, like the family. See the Preface by A. R. Radcliffe-Brown in *African Political Systems,* edited by M. Fortas and E. E. Evans-Pritchard.

16. My colleague Professor Myres S. McDougal and I are applying this general scheme to the study of legal institutions. See H. D. Lasswell and M. S. McDougal, "Legal Education and Public Policy: Professional Training in the Public Interest," *Yale Law Journal,* vol. 52 (1943), pp. 203–95. Reprinted in Lasswell, *The Analysis of Political Behaviour; An Empirical Analysis* (The International Library of Sociology), Part I, Chapter III.

17. The following brief book list may be a guide to the literature concerned with each major value and institution:
    Power: See footnote 13.
    Respect: W. Lloyd Warner and Paul S. Lunt, *The Social Life of a Modern Community.*

Affection: Ernest W. Burgess and Harvey J. Locke, *The Family: From Institution to Companionship.*

Rectitude: William Graham Sumner, *Folkways.*

Well-being: Arthur Newsholme, *Evolution of Preventive Medicine.*

Wealth: Blodgett, *Comparative Economic Systems.*

Enlightenment: Karl Mannheim, *Man and Society in an Age of Reconstruction* (Part IV).

Skill: A. M. Carr-Saunders and P. A. Wilson, *The Professions.*

18. Bertrand Russell, *Power: A New Social Analysis.*

CHAPTER II

1. Concerning the concept of culture, see Bronislav Malinowski, "Culture," vol. 4, *Encyclopaedia of the Social Sciences* (1931), pp. 621–45; Ruth Benedict, *Patterns of Culture;* Clyde Kluckhohn and William H. Kelly, "The Concept of Culture," in *The Science of Man in the World Crisis,* pp. 78–106; A. L. Kroeber, *Configurations of Culture Growth,* ch. 11; P. A. Sorokin, *Social and Cultural Dynamics* (vol. IV); J. S. Plant, *Personality and the Culture Pattern.*

2. Harold Lamb, *Genghis Khan;* B. Y. Vladimirstov, *The Life of Chingis Khan* (Tr. by Prince Mirsky).

3. Miriam Beard, *A History of the Business Man.*

4. J. F. S. Ross, *Parliamentary Representation.*

5. Harold J. Laski, *Studies in Law and Politics,* pp. 181–201.

6. J. Donald Kingsley, *Representative Bureaucracy, an Interpretation of the British Civil Service.*

7. See the forthcoming study by Gabriel Almond, *Wealth and Politics in New York.*

8. Prediction techniques have been applied to many aspects of human response. See Paul Horst and collaborators, *The Prediction of Human Adjustment; a Survey of Logical Problems and Research Techniques with Illustrative Applications to Problems of Vocational Selection, School Success, Marriage and Crime* (Bulletin 48, Social Science Research Council). The transmission of political roles from generation to generation within a family has been studied to some extent, but scarcely with the care of

such monographs as those devoted to biological transmissions, except for monarchs (e.g., Franz J. Kallmann, *The Genetics of Schizophrenia*).

9. The formulation appears in H. D. Lasswell, *Psychopathology and Politics*.

CHAPTER III

1. On the self, see especially George Herbert Mead, *Mind, Self and Society*. Recent social psychology has moved increasingly in this direction, as in Muzafer Sherif and Hadley Cantril, *The Psychology of Ego-Involvements*.

2. This applies the basic postulate of response, the I:D ratio, which expresses the ratio of indulgence to deprivation and states the principle that response maximizes net indulgence over deprivation. Under the impact of behaviorism the older "pleasure-pain" postulate is often rephrased as "abolishing stimuli" in modern systems of psychology. Unconscious as well as conscious dimensions are included, and in this way equivalency is achieved with the Benthamite "calculus of felicity."

3. See H. D. Lasswell, "Collective Autism as a Consequence of Culture Contact: Notes on Religious Training and the Peyote Cult at Taos," *Zeitschrift für Sozialforschung*, vol. 4 (1935), pp. 232–46; Clyde Kluckhohn, "Navaho Witchcraft," *Papers of the Peabody Museum of American Archeology and Ethnology*, Harvard University, vol. XXII, pp. 33–72, 145–49. Responses to deprivation may be predominantly *object orientations, adjustive thinking, autistic reactions* or *somatic reactions*. (They may involve one or more values and institutions.) See the forthcoming study of *Anomie* by Sebastian DeGrazia.

4. On the political pattern referred to, consult William T. R. Fox, *The Super-Powers*.

5. The literature on middle-class ambitiousness is large. A methodologically interesting application of contextual analysis is found in Bruce Lannes Smith, "The Political Communication Specialist of Our Times," in *Propaganda, Communication, and Public Opinion; a Comprehensive Reference Guide*, by B. L. Smith, H. D. Lasswell and R. D. Casey, pp. 31–73.

6. See part 5, section A, of the volume cited in footnote 14. In general, on social mobility and power consult: P. A. Sorokin, *Social Mobility;* Jules Kornis, *L'Homme d'état: Analyse de l'esprit politique.*

7. For example: John G. Heinberg, "The Personnel Structure of French Cabinets," *American Political Science Review,* vol. 33 (1939), pp. 267–78; "State Legislators," in *Annals of the American Academy of Political and Social Science,* vol. 195 (1938), pp. 1–252; Leo C. Rosten, *The Washington Correspondents;* Sigmund Neumann, "The Political Lieutenant," in *Permanent Revolution; the Total State in a World at War,* pp. 73–95.

8. Specific studies are: Werner Sombart, *Der Proletarische Sozialismus* (vol. 2); Hans Gerth, "The Nazi Party: Its Leadership and Composition," *American Journal of Sociology,* 45 (1940), pp. 517–41; Max Nomad, *Rebels and Renegades;* Julien Benda, *The Treason of the Intellectuals;* Hendrik de Man, *Die Intellektuellen und der Sozialismus;* G. P. Gooch, *History and the Historians in the Nineteenth Century.*

9. Alfred Adler's *Individual Psychology* put heavy stress on compensations against organic inferiority as a major dynamism of personality. Eduard C. Lindeman phrased the hypothesis with his customary skill in *The Meaning of Adult Education:* "We are slowly coming to see that all 'power-grabbers' and dictators who reach out for unusual power are in reality compensating for inner deficiencies of their personalities."

10. For a compendious review of research, see Marian E. Breckenridge and E. Lee Vincent, *Child Development; Physical and Psychological Growth through the School Years;* Gardner Murphy, *Personality.*

11. The detailed study of comparative politics has barely begun. Beginnings are made in Ruth Benedict, *Chrysanthemum and the Sword;* P. Kecskemeti and N. Leites, "Some Psychological Hypotheses on Nazi Germany," *The Library of Congress, Washington, D.C., Experimental Division for the Study of War Time Communications,* Document No. 60 (1945), 104 pp.; Geoffrey Gorer, "Themes in Japanese Culture," *Transactions of the New York Academy of Sciences,* vol. 5 (1943), pp. 106–24; Weston La-Barre, "Some Observations on Character Structure in the Orient.

I. The Japanese," *Psychiatry*, vol. 8 (1945), pp. 319–42; "II. The Chinese," *ibid.*, vol. 9 (1946), pp. 215–37; Geoffrey Gorer, *The American People; A Study in National Character*.

12. George E. G. Catlin undertook to formulate a general theory in *The Science and Method of Politics*.

13. A guide to "pathographies" is provided by Wilhelm Lange-Eichbaum, *Genie, Irrsinn und Ruhm*.

14. T. W. Hutchinson, *The Significance and Basic Postulates of Economic Theory*, footnote, page 124, referring to Frank H. Knight, *Risk, Uncertainty, and Profit*.

15. A clear instance: Milton Friedman, "Lange on Price Flexibility and Employment: A Methodological Criticism," *American Economic Review*, vol. 36 (1946), pp. 613–31.

CHAPTER IV

1. See Chapters 6, 7 and 8 in H. D. Lasswell, *Psychopathology and Politics*.

2. Joseph de Maistre, *Essai sur le Principe Générateur des Constitutions Politiques*.

3. Developed in vol. XIX of the collected works of Saint-Simon.

4. A. Lawrence Lowell, *Public Opinion in War and Peace*, ch. 7.

5. E. Kretschmer, *Physique and Character*.

6. W. H. Sheldon, S. S. Stevens, W. B. Tucker, *The Varieties of Human Physique;* W. H. Sheldon and S. S. Stevens, *The Varieties of Temperament*.

7. Beginning with Freud, psychoanalytic characterology was advanced by Karl Abraham and Sandor Ferenczi; and more recently by Wilhelm Reich, Franz Alexander, Theodore Reik and Karen Horney.

8. See especially, Karl Abraham, *Selected Papers*, Anna Freud, *The Ego and the Mechanisms of Defense*, Sigmund Freud, *The Problem of Anxiety*.

9. One of the neglected fields of political research is the interplay of office and personality.

10. On observational standpoints see H. D. Lasswell, *World Politics and Personal Insecurity*, ch. 1.

11. Despite the richness of detailed knowledge about agitational and other political figures, modern methods are rarely used to study them. An exception is Harold Zink, "A Case Study of a Political Boss," *Psychiatry*, vol. 1 (1938), pp. 527–33. This deals with David Curtis Stephenson, head of the Ku Klux Klan in seventeen Middle Western states. See also L. Smith, "Aaron Burr," *Psychoanalytic Quarterly*, vol. 12 (1943), pp. 67–99; Bingham Dai, "Divided Loyalty in War," *Psychiatry*, vol. 7 (1944), pp. 327–40; John S. White, "The Character Development of Ernest Psichari," *Psychiatry*, vol. 7 (1944), pp. 409–23; Ernst Harms, *Psychologie u. Psychiatrie der Conversion*, pp. 97–8; J. R. Rees (editor), *The Case of Rudolf Hess, A Problem in Diagnosis and Forensic Psychiatry;* G. M. Gilbert, *Nuremberg Diary*.

12. Lively psychological sketches of the bureaucrat abound in literature, one of the most imaginative being the famous Buddhist tale for children in which heaven is presented as a huge bureaucracy (*Monkey*). On the "bureaucratic culture pattern" see W. C. MacLeod, *The Origin and History of Politics*. Max Weber's classical analysis of bureaucracy is available in English (translated by H. H. Gerth and C. Wright Mills) *From Max Weber: Essays in Sociology*, ch. 8. See also Daniel Warnotte, "Bureaucratie et fonctionnairisms," *Revue de l'Institut de Sociologie*, vol. 17 (1937), pp. 219–60. Careers in the U.S. Civil Service are summed up in Arthur W. MacMahon and John D. Millett, *Federal Administrators; a Biographical Approach to the Problem of Departmental Management*.

13. Irrespective of his "temperament" and "physique" hypotheses, Kretschmer shows remarkable skill in painting political types. See *The Psychology of Men of Genius*, chs. 9, 10, 11.

CHAPTER V

1. Suggestive studies on drugs and society are: *Studies of Compulsive Drinkers. Part I. Case Histories* by Herman Wortis and Leonard R. Sillman, *Part II. Psychological Test Results* by Florence Halpern, edited by Jane F. Cushman and Carney Landis; Omer C. Stewart, "Washo-Northern Paiute Peyotism; a Study in Acculturation," *University of California Publications in American Archeology and Ethnology*, vol. 40 (1944), pp. vi, 63–142.

2. However an exhaustive guide to the German literature is Wilhelm Lange-Eichbaum, *Genie, Irrsinn und Ruhm*.

3. Iknaton has been studied by James H. Breasted, *Development of Religion and Thought in Ancient Egypt*, and *History of Egypt*.

4. Benj. Whichcote, *Moral and Religious Aphorisms*.

5. J. R. Lowell, *Biglow Papers*, II.

6. Friedrich Meinecke has made the most thorough analysis of the conscious conflicts between morals and power in *Die Idee der Staatsräson in der neueren Geschichte*.

7. In this connection see especially Franz Alexander and H. Staub, *The Criminal, the Judge and the Public;* William Healy, *The Individual Delinquent;* William Healy and Augusta Bronner, *New Light on Delinquency and Its Treatment*. On guilt and society, consult J. C. Flugel, *Man, Morals and Society*.

8. Information about the role of violence in human affairs can be obtained in Quincy Wright, *A Study of War* (2 vols.), and in P. A. Sorokin, *Social and Cultural Dynamics* (vol. III). On violence as a tactic of power, see, for example, E. Kohn-Bramstedt, *Dictatorship and the Political Police*.

9. See H. D. Lasswell, "The Triple-Appeal Principle: A Contribution of Psychoanalysis to Political and Social Science," *American Journal of Sociology*, vol. 37 (1932), pp. 523–38. Reprinted in Lasswell, *The Analysis of Political Behaviour; An Empirical Approach* (The International Library of Sociology), Part II. B. Chapter I. In this article it was pointed out that persons might be chosen primarily on the basis of *reason, conscience* or *impulse* (free translation for *ego, superego* and *id*). Groups in turn may select on the basis of *expediencies, mores* or *countermores*.

10. On the present state of thinking about the study of courts and judges, see the symposium of reviews by members of the faculty of the Yale Law School in the *Yale Law Journal*, vol. 56 (1947), pp. 1458–73.

11. Note that the expression "manifold of events" which is derived from A. N. Whitehead and Bertrand Russell is taken to include all events capable of being referred to, including the event of referring. All events can be classified for descriptive purposes into

symbol events and nonsymbol events, the first of which *refer,* the second of which do not. An act is a sequence of events which, if completed, passes through *impulse, subjectivity,* to *expression;* subjective and expressive events may occur simultaneously as well as in sequence. In a yet more general perspective, the act arises in *tension* and concludes in *gratification* (the restoration of an initial pattern of relationship taken as the base of comparison; or a new pattern of relationship which is expected to function as an initial pattern in the future). The scientific observer of the acts of another person relies upon indexes which are symbols (words or word equivalents) or nonsymbols (movements of striated or smooth muscle, etc.). It is inconsequential whether he uses "behavioristic" or "nonbehavioristic" terminology, if his definitions and operational rules are explicit. On the general theory of the act, consult George Herbert Mead, especially his *Philosophy of the Act.* An act is "externalized" when the environment is much involved in its completion, "internalized" when the environment is less involved. The term cue refers to the features of the environment that initiate a response. Predispositions are the state of preparation with which a potential responder enters a situation (ready to receive cues). A successful response (from the standpoint of environmental analysis) brings about favorable (indulgent) changes in the value position of the actor. An unsuccessful response, on the contrary, is followed by unfavorable (deprivational) environmental changes. The frame of reference for describing the fact and degree of gratification is interpersonal, and hence calls for the consideration of all parties to the process. Appraisals are made according to certain selected "terminal" patterns (values: categories of gratification, which are given "operational indexes" by observers who occupy a given observational standpoint.)

CHAPTER VI

1. James Bryce, Modern Democracies, ch. 75.
2. Leon J. Saul, "Physiological Effects of Emotional Tensions," in *Personality and the Behavior Disorders; a Handbook Based on Experimental and Clinical Research,* ch. 8.

3. H. Flanders Dunbar, *Emotions and Bodily Changes* (2nd ed.).

4. Refer, for example, to Karen Horney, *Our Inner Conflicts; a Constructive Theory of Neurosis;* Otto Fenichel, *The Psychoanalytic Theory of Neurosis;* Jules H. Masserman, *Behavior and Neurosis; an Experimental Psychoanalytic Approach to Psychobiologic Principles.* In our culture anxiety is often traced to such focal incidents as the imposing of deprivations by the primary environment in connection with infantile masturbation, weaning or cleanliness training. James Clark Moloney was surprised to see that infantile masturbation did not occur among the babies of Okinawa: James Clark Moloney, "Psychiatric Observations in Okinawa Shima," *Psychiatry,* vol. 8 (1945), pp. 391–99. Margaret E. Fries has devised promising methods for the study of early reactions. See also the researches of Margaret Ribble and Phyllis Greenacre (conveniently summarized in *The Psychoanalytic Study of the Child,* vol. 1 [1942]).

5. C. B. Chisholm, "The Psychiatry of Enduring Peace and Social Progress," *The William Alanson White Memorial Lectures.*

6. See Gregory Zilboorg and George W. Henry, *A History of Medical Psychology.*

7. On semantics see especially Charles W. Morris, *Signs, Language and Behavior;* Ernst Cassirer, *Language and Myth;* Lawrence S. Kubie, "Body Symbolization and the Development of Language," *Psychoanalytic Quarterly,* vol. 3 (1934), pp. 430–44; C. K. Ogden and I. A. Richards, *The Meaning of Meaning;* Edward Sapir, "Communication," *Encyclopaedia of the Social Sciences,* vol. 4 (1931), pp. 78–80; "Language," *ibid.,* vol. 9 (1933), pp. 155–68; "Symbolism," *ibid.,* vol. 14 (1934), pp. 492–95; Alfred Korzybski, *Science and Sanity: An Introduction to Non-Aristotelian Systems and General Semantics;* Harry Stack Sullivan, "Peculiarity of Thought in Schizophrenia," *American Journal of Psychiatry,* vol. 5 (1925–26), pp. 21–86; Robert E. Park, "Symbiosis and Socialization: A Frame of Reference for the Study of Society," *The American Journal of Sociology,* vol. 45 (1939), pp. 1–25.

8. Notably Charles E. Merriam and Beardsley Ruml.

9. Robert S. Lynd posed the issue sharply in *Knowledge for What?* See also Karl Mannheim, *Man and Society in an Age of Reconstruction,* parts IV, V, VI.

10. John W. Burgess, *Reminiscences of an American Scholar.*

11. All means other than military are often summed up in the term "political." During war the terminology is adapted to various combinations, as when "psychological warfare" covers not only words as propaganda but the management of other instruments chiefly to gain symbolic effects. (An assassination, or the use of "screamers," with a view to obtaining an effect out of proportion to the stimulus.)

12. Quoted by R. W. Emerson, *Essay on Politics.*

13. Shrewd observers have long recognized the substitutive relation-ship among activities. Bakunin, for instance, wrote in *Dieu et l'état,* "There are but three ways for the populace to escape its wretched lot. The first two are by the routes of the wine-shop or the church; the third is by that of the social revolution." See also H. D. Lasswell and Dorothy Blumenstock, *World Revolutionary Propaganda; a Chicago Study,* part V, and the classic research by Paul Lazarsfeld and H. Zeisl, "Die Arbeitslosen von Marienthal," *Psychol. Monographen* (1933).

14. Oliver Garceau, *The Political Life of the American Medical Association.*

15. On legal education and the role of the lawyer, see A. A. Berle, Jr., "Modern Legal Profession," *Encyclopaedia of the Social Sciences,* vol. 9 (1933), pp. 340–45; Fred Rodell, *Woe Unto You, Lawyers!;* Jerome Frank, "A Plea for Lawyer-Schools," *Yale Law Journal,* vol. 52 (1947), pp. 1303–44; Myres S. McDougal, "The Law School of the Future: From Legal Realism to Policy Science in the World Community," *Yale Law Journal,* vol. 52 (1947), pp. 1345–55.

16. Elaborated in Carl L. Becker, *Every Man His Own Historian.*

17. R. L. Stevenson, *Familiar Studies of Men and Books,* V.

18. See the *Bulletin of the Atomic Scientists.*

19. *The Report of the Royal Commission* (Canada), June 27, 1946, pp. 1–733.

20. S. d'Irsay, *Histoire des Universités.*

21. An example: Haret, *Mécanique Sociale.*

22. However, see the perspectives opened by John von Neumann and Oskar Morgenstern, *Theory of Games and Economic Behaviour.*

23. In the field of law see the precise, elegant and circumscribed work of Underhill Moore and Charles C. Callahan, *Law and Learning Theory: A Study in Legal Control.*

CHAPTER VII

1. *Associated Press v. United States,* 326 United States Reports 1 to 20 (1945). For context see Zechariah Chafee, Jr., *Government and Mass Communications* (2 vols.).

2. Irving Fisher in *American Economic Review* (Supplement, March, 1919).

3. Gaetano Mosca, *The Ruling Class,* ch. 3.

4. William Penn, *Fruits of Solitude.*

5. *New York Journal and Weekly Register,* Sept. 27, 1787.

6. *Life and Letters of Washington Irving,* edited by P. M. Irving, vol. 1, ch. 11. Also Paul Valéry, "L'avenir de l'esprit européenne," *Société des Nations, Institut International de cooperation Intellectuelle* (1933): "Je considère la politique, l'action politique, les formes politiques comme des valeurs inférieures de l'esprit." For a vigorous statement of the "price of politics" which is alleged to be "far too high for the average human being's endurance," see Max Ascoli, "War Aims and America's Aims," *Social Research,* vol. 8 (1941), pp. 267–82. Gerald Heard speaks of the "domesticians" who love "familiarity, security and the sense of being right and led," in *Man the Master.*

7. Joan Riviere, "On the Genesis of Psychical Conflict in Earliest Infancy," *International Journal of Psychoanalysis,* vol. 17 (1936), pp. 395–422. Among the studies of indulgence, deprivation and response are: Gregory Bateson and Margaret Mead, "Balinese Character; a Photographic Analysis," *Special Publications of the N.Y. Academy of Science;* K. Lewin, R. Lippitt, S. K. Escalona, "An Experimental Study of the Effect of Democratic and Authoritarian Group Atmospheres," *Studies in Topological and Vector Psychology,* No. 1 (*Studies in Child Welfare,* vol. XVI, no. 3).

8. Sigmund Freud, *The Problem of Anxiety.*

9. Some differences in research findings can quite probably be attributed to the position in the social structure of the subjects (and

the observers). Breckenridge and Vincent point out in their *Child Development* that Levy and Tulchin drew their subjects from lower occupational classes, whereas Goodenough, Jersild and Dawe studied more privileged children. Boys in the more privileged classes are said to be more often spoiled than girls. On voice and personality see, for example, *Language, Culture and Personality; Essays in Memory of Edward Sapir,* edited by Leslie Spier, A. Irving Hallowell, Stanley S. Newman; Miriam Rose Bonner, "Changes in Speech Pattern under Emotional Stress," *American Journal of Psychology,* vol. LVI (1943), pp. 262–73.

10. See especially, Harry Stack Sullivan, *Conceptions of Modern Psychiatry, the First William Alanson White Memorial Lecture.* Sullivan (and Erich Fromm, *Escape from Freedom*) has performed a valuable function in challenging Freud's conception of narcissism. Trigant Burrow has long sought for a reliable means of discovering the "social image" as distinct from "reality." See Hans Syz, "Phylopathology," *Encyclopaedia of Psychology,* edited by Philip Lawrence Harriman.

11. Ryder Translation.

12. Georges Sorel, *Réflexions sur la violence.*

13. Gustave E. von Grunebaum, *Medieval Islam,* ch. 5.

14. Wilhelm Reich, *The Mass Psychology of Fascism,* ch. 9. An alert attempt to collect field data on political perspectives when President Roosevelt died is reported by Sebastian de Grazia, "A Note on the Psychological Position of the Chief Executive," *Psychiatry,* vol. 8 (1945), pp. 267–72. De Grazia is making a systematic study of the role of certain early experiences on collective *anomie.* On the nondemocratic personality, see A. H. Maslow, "The Authoritarian Character Structure," *The Journal of Social Psychology,* XVIII (1943), pp. 401–11.

15. See J. C. Flugel's concise summary of Melanie Klein's work in *Man, Morals and Society,* ch. 9.

16. Consult especially E. H. Erikson, "Hitler's Imagery and German Youth," *Psychiatry,* vol. 5 (1942), pp. 475–93; Fritz Redl, "Group Emotion and Leadership," *Psychiatry,* vol. 5 (1942), pp. 573–96; E. H. Erikson, "Childhood and Tradition in Two American Indian Tribes," *The Psychoanalytic Study of the Child,* vol. 1

(1945), pp. 319–50; Edith Buxbaum, "Transference and Group Formation in Children and Adolescents," *ibid.*, vol. 1 (1945), pp. 351–65.

17. *Developmental* profiles can be obtained by the method of interlapping observation. While group B is passing through its third and fourth years, for instance, group A can be followed as it passes through the second and third years, and group C can be described as it goes through the fourth and fifth years.

18. Events along the career line can be observed by scientists directly or indirectly. One of the indirect methods is the document prepared by the subject. See: *The Use of Personal Documents in History, Anthropology and Sociology* by Louis Gottschalk, Clyde Kluckhohn, Robert Angell (Social Science Research Council, Bulletin 53, 1945); *The Use of Personal Documents in Psychological Science* by Gordon W. Allport (Social Science Research Council, Bulletin 49, 1942). Content analysis, or quantitative semantics, is one of the most promising procedures for describing gestures and speech. See B. L. Smith, H. D. Lasswell, R. D. Casey, *Propaganda, Communication and Public Opinion; a Comprehensive Reference Guide,* especially "Describing the Contents of Communications" (pp. 74–94). John Dollard and O. Hobart Mower, "A Method of Measuring Tension in Written Documents," *Journal of Abnormal and Social Psychology,* vol. 42 (1947), pp. 3–32. On some dimensions of the problem, see *A Free and Responsible Press: A General Report on Mass Communication: Newspapers, Radio, Motion Pictures, Magazines and Books,* by The Commission on Freedom of the Press, with a Foreword by Robert M. Hutchins; *Peoples Speaking to Peoples,* by Llewellyn White and Robert D. Leigh.

19. These suggestions recapture Jeremy Bentham's approach to public policy. He wanted legislative enactments subject to review at periodic intervals. In his day the technical problems of measuring social trend were in a most rudimentary state.

CHAPTER VIII

1. See Seymour E. Harris, editor, *The New Economics: Keynes' Influence on Theory and Public Policy.*

2. Among those who seek to connect psychological technique with

the study of economics, see George Katona, *War without Infla-tion,* and John S. Gambs, *Beyond Supply and Demand.* Rensis Likert of the University of Michigan has been applying some of the techniques of modern communication research to this prob-lem in co-operation with government agencies.

3. H. D. Lasswell, *World Politics and Personal Insecurity,* ch. 3.

4. Bernard Brodie, editor, *The Absolute Weapon; Atomic Power and World Order.*

5. The views here are partly in accord with "X" (George Kennan) in "The Sources of Soviet Conduct" in *Foreign Affairs,* vol. 25 (1947), pp. 566–82. We concur in "physical defense"; but we diverge by putting stress upon "psychological offense."

6. See H. D. Lasswell, "The Interrelations of World Organization and Society," *Yale Law Journal,* vol. 55 (1946), pp. 889–909; and *World Politics Faces Economics, with Special Reference to the Future Relations of the United States and Russia,* A Committee for Economic Development Research Study.

7. Irving Hallowell, "Aggression in Salteaux Society," *Psychiatry* 3 (1940), pp. 395–407.

8. This is one of its many dimensions. See N. S. Timasheff, *An In-troduction to the Sociology of Law;* Eugen Ehrlich, *Fundamental Principles of the Sociology of Law;* N. M. Korkunov, *General Theory of Law;* Ranyard West, *Conscience and Society;* Malcolm Sharp, "Aggression: A Study of Values and Law," *Ethics,* vol. LVII (1947), pp. 1–39 (part 2).

9. J. L. Moreno, *Who Shall Survive?* and the journal *Sociometry.*

10. Elton Mayo, *The Social Problems of an Industrial Civilization.*

11. I have discussed this problem with Lawrence K. Frank, in partic-ular. A concise report of the present state of knowledge is in J. P. Guilford, "The Discovery of Aptitude and Achievement Varia-bles," *Science,* vol. 106 (1947), pp. 279–82. See the forthcoming study of democracy by E. A. Shils (London and Chicago).

CHAPTER IX

1. See especially Ernst Kris, "The Covenant of the Gangsters," *Jour-nal of Criminal Psychopathology,* vol. 4 (1943), pp. 445–58; "Some Problems of War Propaganda," *Psychoanalytic Quarterly,* vol. 12

(1943), pp. 381–99; "Danger and Morale," *American Journal of Orthopsychiatry*, vol. XIV (1944), pp. 147–55; "The 'Danger' of Propaganda," *The American Imago*, vol. II (1941), pp. 5–42. Kris has described democratic group formation as one in which identification in the superego is supplemented by ego formation. Improving the intelligence function calls for new techniques of deliberation. E. L. Thorndike, for instance, suggested that all voting be done by "secret ballot after the question and the facts at hand have been presented, but before any discussion" (*Human Nature and the Social Order*, p. 836). Margaret Mead and I have experimented with the "clarifier" in discussion whose task is to interrogate in orderly fashion those who present "facts" or "sides."

2. My assistants were Jesse MacKnight and G. C. Routt. Report eventually to be published.

3. The making and receiving of petitions has usually been recognized as an "obligation" or "right," as well as a tactic of survival. It is explicitly mentioned, for instance, in the code of Hammurabi.

4. See Arthur R. Burns, *The Decline of Competition; a Study of the Evolution of American Industry.*

5. See F. J. Roethlisberger and William J. Dickson, *Management and the Worker;* T. N. Whitehead, *The Industrial Worker* (2 vols.); H. D. Lasswell, *Psychopathology and Politics,* ch. 3, and *Democracy through Public Opinion,* ch. 4. An excellent case study of what happens when there is no insight is "Manager Meets Union: A Case Study in Personal Immaturity," by Joseph M. Goldsen and Lillian Low, in *Human Factors in Management* (ed. by S. D. Hoslett). (This volume is an excellent indication of the present state of thinking among our ablest specialists.)

6. Ernst Kapp, *Greek Foundations of Traditional Logic.*

7. See Morris R. Cohen and Ernest Nagel, *An Introduction to Logic and Scientific Method.*

8. Karen Horney, *Self-Analysis,* especially Chapter 9.

9. Franz Alexander and Thomas M. French, *Psychoanalytic Therapy; Principles and Application,* especially Chapters 2 and 3. Alexander refers to Jean Valjean as an example of what can be accomplished by a corrective emotional experience (pp. 68–70).

10. Albert N. Mayers, "Dug-out Psychiatry," *Psychiatry,* vol. 8 (1945), pp. 383–89.

11. Trigant Burrow has been a pioneer advocate of group therapy. In recent times the most adventurous movements have grown up around J. L. Moreno. See J. L. Moreno, editor, *Group Psychotherapy, a Symposium.*

12. "Alcoholics Anonymous" is meant.

13. See, for instance, the researches on print conducted or instigated by Douglas Waples; the studies of radio by Paul Lazarsfeld, Frank Stanton, Hadley Cantril, Robert Merton, Ernst Kris, Hans Speier; the analyses of film by Dorothy (Blumenstock) Jones, Siegfried Kracauer, Gregory Bateson.

14. Wrote Paul Schilder: "Psychoanalysis should teach us, as judges and law-makers, to see the deep similarity between ourselves and the criminal, and to prevent us from enacting our own criminal instincts in the punishment of the criminal" (*Psychoanalysis Today,* edited by S. Lorand). Even psychoanalytic experience is not enough, since many more or less lengthily analyzed persons unwittingly resume old or conventional attitudes after analysis. Continuous support by the environment of the analytical frame of reference is necessary. The task is that of providing a stream of analytic communication which most effectively provides this support. A new culture pattern is called for.

15. Some of the army and navy training films prepared during World War II served this purpose. One aim of free association is to increase awareness of gestures and their possible significance as evidence of anxiety or composure, and of assertive-nonassertive tendencies, and other traits. Note in this connection the observations made by G. M. Gilbert in *Nuremberg Diary* (e.g. at pp. 185 and 384). See Maurice Krout, *Autistic Gestures;* A. Elkin, *Gesture and Environment.*

16. Margaret Brenman and Morton M. Gill, *Hypnotherapy: A Survey of the Literature,* The Menninger Foundation Monograph Series No. 5.

17. Charles E. Merriam edited a *Civic Training Series* which contains many useful descriptions of prewar conditions.

18. See H. D. Lasswell and M. S. McDougal, "Legal Education and Public Policy: Professional Training in the Public Interest," *Yale Law Journal,* vol. 52 (1943), pp. 203–95. Reprinted in Lasswell, *The Analysis of Political Behaviour; An Empirical Approach* (The International Library of Sociology), Part I, Chapter III.

19. Karl Mannheim, *Man and Society in an Age of Reconstruction,* parts IV and V.

20. Not "logical" thinking in the sense of inquiry. See John Dewey, *Logic: The Theory of Inquiry.*

21. When historians undertake explanations, they become scientists. See Frederick J. Teggart, *Theory and Processes of History.*

22. H. D. Lasswell, *World Politics and Personal Insecurity,* ch. 1; Felix Kaufmann, *Methodology of the Social Sciences.*

CHAPTER X

1. For the expectation of progress consult J. B. Bury, *The Idea of Progress;* Carl L. Becker, *The Heavenly City of the Eighteenth Century Philosophers.*

2. Leon Trotsky's ideas are repeated in his posthumously published *Stalin; an Appraisal of the Man and His Influence.*

3. Side by side with the myth according to Marx is the myth according to Mises (and Hayek).

4. Franz Neumann, *Behemoth: The Structure and Practice of National Socialism, 1933–1944.*

5. H. D. Lasswell, "The Garrison State," *The American Journal of Sociology,* vol. 46 (1941), pp. 455–68. Reprinted in Lasswell, *The Analysis of Political Behaviour, An Empirical Approach* (The International Library of Sociology), Part II. A., Chapter II.

6. Kurt Koffka, *Principles of Gestalt Psychology* and *The Growth of the Mind;* Kurt Lewin, *Principles of Topological Psychology* and "Frontiers in Group Dynamics," *Human Relations,* vol. 1 (1947), pp. 5–41.

7. Walter B. Cannon, *The Wisdom of the Body.*

8. B. Malinowski, *A Scientific Theory of Culture and Other Essays.*

9. Myres S. McDougal, "Future Interests Restated: Tradition versus Clarification and Reform," *Harvard Law Review,* 55 (1942), pp.

1077 ff. Walton H. Hamilton, "Property," *Encyclopaedia of the Social Sciences,* vol. 12 (1934), pp. 528–38.

10. Varying degrees of liberation from mythology are represented in J. A. Schumpeter, *Democracy, Capitalism and Socialism;* and R. H. Blodgett, *Comparative Economic Systems.* A fundamental study of the impact of technology on man is in course of publication by Georges Friedmann (Paris).

INDEX

245